> *We all live with the objective of being happy; our lives are all different and yet the same.*
> **Anne Frank**

Within these pages, you will uncover some of the most effective and powerful information that you need to put to work in your organisation, starting today – no matter what business you are in.

> *Don't make assumptions. Find the courage to ask questions and to express what you really want. Communicate with others as clearly as you can to avoid misunderstandings, sadness and drama. With just this one agreement, you can completely transform your life.*
> **Miguel Angel Ruiz**

Ever Say DIE – Common Sense Business Sense – *Mui Li*

First published in 2012 by
Ecademy Press
48 St Vincent Drive, St Albans, Herts, AL1 5SJ
info@ecademy-press.com
www.ecademy-press.com

Printed and bound by Lightning Source in the UK and USA
Design by Martin Coote

Printed on acid-free paper from managed forests. This book is printed on demand, so no copies will be remaindered or pulped.

ISBN 978-1-907722-98-1

The right of Mui Li to be identified as the author of this work has been inserted in accordance with sections 77 and 78 of the Copyright Designs and Patents Act 1988.

A CIP catalogue record for this book is available from the British Library.

This book is available online and all good bookstores.

A note on Accessibility: This book has been designed to be readable and legible for the widest possible audience, however if you require the book in an alternative format please contact Mui. *mui@muikaleadership.com*

Ever Say

Dedication

To my family, friends and to the thousands of participants I have worked with, who have provided me with invaluable insights into their worlds.

Acknowledgements

With appreciation and many thanks to:

Karen Murphy, my business partner and friend, who provides invaluable expertise, energy and support; *John Wells*, my partner, who is unconditional in all he gives; *Ruth Overton* for her outstanding knowledge and commitment to inclusion; and *Lara Farnham* for her invaluable images and creative talents. To *Jan Farnham*, from whom I have learnt a lot about myself.

Foreword

Diversity, inclusion and equality are challenging areas for many of us, in both our personal and professional lives. To have an understanding and confidence, when it comes to understanding difference, can see us lead successful businesses and live very enriched lives. Yet, so many of us are frightened by the notion of difference; a lack of understanding, and being fearful of finding out, can lead to tension, conflict, disharmony and discrimination, and perhaps, at its worst, war.

I met Mui many years ago, while we were both working with a group of police officers delivering a two-day diversity workshop. Mui stood out. She had the ability to help everyone feel at ease and let down any barriers they had regarding what they were about to do. She helped them to feel safe.

Many years later, I was fortunate to have the opportunity to work with Mui again. Yet again, she had the same amazing impact. Her ability to take a subject that experience told me many people felt fearful of, and create an environment where others could explore, engage, challenge and learn, was truly incredible. She has helped so many people, including myself, to raise their awareness, to seek to understand, and to ask questions, where they may previously have felt uncomfortable or uncertain. She does not seek to blame or chastise, and, in so doing, has helped educate, dispel myths, and create more understanding and harmony than anyone else I have ever seen working in this field.

I am now very fortunate to have Mui as my business partner, and my very good friend. We run Muika Leadership together, and deliver training to help others in the fields of leadership, diversity, inclusion and equality. Without fail, every programme that Mui designs and/or delivers receives outstanding feedback. She has now finally acted upon the feedback she has been given time and time again by those attending her programmes and by her friends and colleagues – write a book that can help people, in the way that she does in her workshops. And here it is.

I believe this book will be invaluable to all those who perform leadership roles within business and to all those who want to understand and live more harmoniously with others who they perceive are different. Mui has made this subject, through her book, accessible to everyone. It is straightforward yet challenging, informative but not patronising. In my view, this is an area we cannot be ignorant of, and with the aid of this book, we no longer need be.

Karen Murphy

Contents

Chapter One – What is Diversity, Equality & Inclusion?   **1**
- Definitions

Chapter Two – The Public & Private Sectors   **7**
- Is there a difference in what they do?
- Ethical/Moral Case – Business Case – Legal Case

Chapter Three – Responding to Difference   **13**
- 6 Types of Response
- Prejudice – Gordon Allport
- Types of Collusion

Chapter Four – Equalities Legislation   **19**
The Equality Act 2010
Rationale for 2010 Act
Getting Behind the Words
- Harassment
- Victimisation
- Institutional Discrimination
- Discrimination: by association; by perception; direct; indirect; multiple discrimination; in-group discrimination
- Positive Action; Affirmative Action; Positive Discrimination
- A Racist Incident; Racism
- A Genuine Occupational Requirement (GOR)
- Stereotypes
- Archetypes

Chapter Five – Exploring the Nine Protected Characteristics in   **29**
the Equality Act 2010
1. Age
2. Disability
3. Gender Reassignment
4. Marriage/Civil Partnership
5. Pregnancy and Maternity
6. Race
7. Religion or Belief
8. Sex
9. Sexual Orientation – Bisexual; Gay; Heterosexual; Lesbian

Chapter Six – Not in the Nine Protected Characteristics but   **51**
Equally Important
- Socioeconomics – Class – Poverty

Chapter Seven – The Financial Costs of Discrimination   **53**
- Examples of discrimination cases across the Nine Protected
  Characteristics

Chapter Eight – 'The way we do things around here'   **59**
- Unwritten Rules
- Values and Beliefs, based on diverse experiences
- The socialisation process
- Assumptions – Behaviour – Outcomes

Chapter Nine – Culture   **65**
- The Power of Cultural Beliefs
- Cross Cultural Communication

Chapter Ten – The Learning Cycle   **73**
- From Unconscious Incompetence to Unconscious
  Competence
- Balance – Unbalanced – Searching – New Balance

Chapter Eleven – Structures & Systems – What's Happening   **81**
in Your Organisation?
- Organisational Policies and Practices
- Diversity and Inclusion Strategy and Performance
  Management Framework
- Performance Measures
- Steering Committee
- Monitoring to stop discrimination
- Monitoring Form

Chapter Twelve – Self-Assessment   **97**
- Further questions for consideration
- Climate Mapping
- Displays

Chapter Thirteen – Self-Assessment   **103**
Further consideration about culture – assumptions,
behaviour & outcomes
- Eleven point guide to successful cross-cultural
  communication
- Approaches to working in a culturally competent workplace
- Examples of differences between cultures

Chapter Fourteen – Delivering Training   **107**
- Muika Leadership and Focussed Thinking
- The Trainer/Facilitator: Self-awareness – social awareness

Chapter Fifteen – Equalities Legislation   **111**
- Background Information to The Equality Act 2010
- Websites for Further Reference and Information

Chapter One

What are Diversity, Inclusion and Equality?

❝ *Diversity may be the hardest thing for a society to live with,*
and perhaps the most dangerous thing for a society to be without.
William Sloane Coffin, Jr.

• **Definitions**

Introduction

I have chosen to begin this book with the way I see the concepts of diversity, inclusion and equality. I visit organisations or look at their policies on websites, and often find a disparity between the written words and the actual practice. Moreover, I want to lay out before the reader just exactly what these powerful terms mean to me.

What is Diversity?

Diversity is not a textbook issue; it is about demonstrating inclusive practices. The term Diversity is used to draw out and address the differences that lie within the broad headings of inclusion and equality. Moreover, in order to implement inclusion and equality, it is important to have an understanding of diversity.

Diversity is about the uniqueness of an individual; for example, when looking at a person's ethnicity, it is useful to take into account their age, disability, class, language, sex, sexual orientation, socioeconomic status, as this is their '3-D' unique self. Diversity is also about the uniqueness of groups of individuals, and the differences between people. When we look at diversity, we also become aware of the broad spectrum of similarities that we share.

People have different perceptions, attitudes and awareness about what inclusion and equality are or what they ought to be; there are different levels of commitment to them. This is demonstrated in our assumptions and behaviour towards each other, adult to adult, as well as through an organisation's recruitment practices, performance management, promotion, redundancy, resources and displays etc. These practices offer opportunities for employers and employees to ensure that direct and indirect discrimination does not take place, either wittingly or unwittingly.

Additionally, for this to be achieved, it is vital that all those working together build on their existing good practice, and, together, critically monitor, review and evaluate the implementation of diversity, inclusion and equality.

From an early age, we learn about differences, and become capable of assigning values to them, positive or negative, depending on the belief and value system we absorb through the families and communities we are brought up in; the formal and informal education systems we have experienced; traditions, customs, beliefs, religion and the media.

Individuals and groups may well have biased and stereotyped views of each other, some of which might be positive, helping to enhance the self-worth of the other individual or group, whilst others may be negative stereotypes and assumptions, which can cause serious conflict and harm. By ensuring that issues such as difference, similarity and injustice are considered and acknowledged, we hope to encourage all those working together to build a greater understanding and appreciation of other people different to themselves, rather than allowing differences to divide and separate.

If adults learn to discuss, think and talk about differences and the common ground between people and groups, they may be able to recognise how those differences can be associated with inequality, and then consider appropriate ways of challenging behaviours, which can lead to injustice, prejudice and discrimination. We can all say things without thinking, but it is vital that each of us acquires meaningful knowledge about diversity, so that we can use our awareness for our own benefit and that of our colleagues.

A workplace ethos, which favours some groups or individuals over others is discriminatory, and will not ensure that everyone feels recognised, valued and respected.

Diversity

Individuals/groups that may experience discrimination because of their difference, such as:

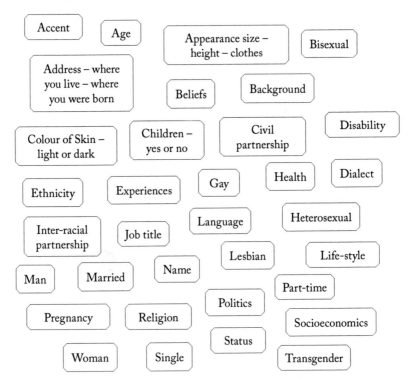

Accent

Age

Appearance size – height – clothes

Bisexual

Address – where you live – where you were born

Beliefs

Background

Colour of Skin – light or dark

Children – yes or no

Civil partnership

Disability

Ethnicity

Experiences

Gay

Health

Dialect

Inter-racial partnership

Job title

Language

Heterosexual

Man

Married

Name

Lesbian

Life-style

Pregnancy

Religion

Politics

Part-time

Woman

Single

Status

Socioeconomics

Transgender

Out of this wide expanse of diversity, the Equality Act 2010 has recognised nine areas, henceforth referred to as the Nine Protected Characteristics, which it deems to require specific protection under the law. These are

1. Age
2. Disability
3. Gender Reassignment
4. Marriage/Civil Partnership
5. Pregnancy and Maternity
6. Race
7. Religion or Belief
8. Sex
9. Sexual Orientation – Bisexual; Gay; Heterosexual; Lesbian

(These areas will be covered in depth in Chapter Five)

What is Inclusion?

"You can be part of a group, but not feel included – you know in yourself when you are truly included, just by how it feels"
Participant at Muika Leadership workshop

Inclusion:

- Is about the positive assumption that everyone has a right to be part of what's going on, as well as behaviour and practices;
- Promotes a culture of equality of opportunity and high achievement for all, by encouraging the development of more flexible attitudes, policies and everyday practices, designed to get the best from each person. Also promotes organisational cohesion and integration, through understanding of and respect for others;
- Inclusive organisations understand and celebrate diversity.

What is Equality?

Equality is equal treatment according to NEEDS – the challenge for all of us is the identification of NEEDS.

An equal and inclusive organisation recognises people's different needs, situations and goals, and removes the barriers that limit what people can do and can be.

This definition recognises that:

- Equality is an issue for everyone;
- We don't all start from the same position, and, to create a fair workplace, we must recognise and respond appropriately to different needs;
- There is an interaction between characteristics, such as age and disability, gender and ethnicity, etc;
- There is, for example, an interaction between diversity, inclusion and socioeconomic status.

The Equality Duty to:

- eliminate unlawful discrimination, harassment and victimisation, and any other conduct prohibited by the Act;
- advance equality of opportunity between people who share a protected characteristic and people who do not share it; and foster good relations between people who share a protected characteristic and people who do not share it.

http://www.homeoffice.gov.uk/equalities

http://www.equalityhumanrights.com/legal-and-policy/equality-act/what-is-the-equality-act/

I would add to this the importance of monitoring and reviewing – collecting information, analysing it, and evaluating the effectiveness of policies, procedures and practices, to help establish whether discrimination occurs.

This book is intended to act as a reference point for any questions you may have, with regard to diversity, inclusion and equality; whether you are Chief Executive, Non Executive Director, Chief Operating Officer, Senior Leader, Human Resource Director, or someone who would simply like to know more. I believe its contents are significant for all, and should not be open to a select few. I know there will be information at varying degrees for all people. Some of you may well be thoroughly aware of much contained within, while others of you will find plenty that is new, and lots to inform and support you.

Chapter Two

The Public & Private Sectors

> **"** *Diversity is the one true thing we all have in common.*
> *Celebrate it every day.*
> Michel de Montaigne

- **Is there a difference in what they do?**
- **Ethical/Moral Case – Business Case – Legal Case**

The public and private sectors – is there a difference in what they do?
In all public sectors, there are numerous policies and processes in place which focus on diversity, inclusion and equality – the challenge is in providing evidence that demonstrates that the policy is put into practice. Equally, in the private sector, I have found many examples where companies have appeared to be proactive; spending huge budgets on advertising their positive adherence to diversity and equality. Yet, in so many, a search on their website can be an onerous task if you enter either of those key words.

In some organisations, diversity and equality is about helpful little tips for avoiding faux pas should you happen to be posted to a branch in some foreign clime. For others, it is simply that they are a global company and assumed to be a high level equality provider – not necessarily the case. Some miss the point that diversity is diverse, and exists within and without all places, where we live and work. For some, it can be merely about advertising their prominence in the diversity strand, which is currently in fashion. For example, recently, several reports have focussed on women in the workplace and the 'glass ceiling'. Thus, several companies want to display how they are free of gender bias, yet may be uncomfortable with discussions around issues of transgender or sexual orientation. With inclusion firmly rooted, a company embraces all diversity, at all times.

The public sector may have a head start in requiring adherence to diversity and equality policies and practice but there is no reason to believe that this is its natural or only home. The multiple reasons for ensuring a place of work is diverse, inclusive and equality-based, are as relevant in the private as in the public sector.

Private Sector & Public Sector
Anti-discrimination statutes apply to both sectors; however, the discrepancy lies within the fact that whilst the public sector is mandated to promote the requirements of the Equality Act 2010 (the Act), the private sector is encouraged to ensure good equality practice. The Discrimination Law Review (DLR) has 30 pages about 'public sector equality duties', but only four pages on 'promoting good equality practice in the private sector'. Can there really be such a vast discrepancy of actual need?

The Challenges for the Private Sector

Every smart organisation understands that everything they desire, including increasing their profits and being the best place to work, is down to their ability to be successful, not just at leadership, but also diversity and inclusion – and the really smart ones are honest enough to admit there's a big gap between leadership, diversity and inclusive behaviours that they and others in their business are currently demonstrating, and what they need to understand and then demonstrate to achieve the commercial success they want.

In spite of having equalities legislation since the 1960s, the lack of understanding and implementation of inclusive practices is alarming, as are the consequences for the individuals and organisations, and of course society as a whole.

For Example – House of Commons Treasury Committee, Women in the City –Tenth Report of Session 2009-10

It appears that the problem lies, not in the existence of flexible working policies, but with getting permission to use the available policies, especially at senior levels. While virtually every City firm has adequate policies for supporting flexible working and diversity, the disconnect is in their take-up and implementation.

So, organisations can have policies, and espouse values about being inclusive, but do they really understand what they need to do, and know how to do it?

More recently, there has been a focus on the number of women on boards. The Female FTSE Board Report 2010 found that:

- overall, the percentage of women on FTSE 100 boards is 12.5%, showing a three-year plateau;
- only 13% of new appointments were female;
- 52.4% of FTSE 250 companies have no women on their boards.

A government review by Lord Davies in February 2011 called for 25% female board representation by 2015 – but the report stops short of a mandatory quota. In July 2011, head hunters instead opted for a voluntary code of conduct, drawn up by executive search firms, representing 19 leading companies in the sector. This code has seven key principles of best practice which include setting diversity goals, defining the client brief to balance experience with relevant skills, and giving support during the selection process.

Muika Leadership has written extensively about the issue of quotas, in relation to the pros and cons. Lord Davies calls for 25% female board representation – what do organisations need to do about this? I believe it is about putting policy into practice – most organisations acknowledge the business benefits of having a diverse workforce.

Private sector organisations, who implement inclusion and equality practices, are more likely to be at a competitive advantage. The return on investment for employers, who are willing to tackle and challenge the current status quo, could be huge. Organisations, which are seen to be employers of choice, have access to a larger talent pool, and hence would be better positioned to represent the needs of customers and communities. The focus of Lord Davies' report is on gender diversity, which is a step in the right direction; still, we must also recognise that women – as with men – are not a homogenous group, but are from diverse cultures, and thus have different experiences. The challenge is how to ensure that everyone understands what diversity and inclusion means, and is able to put the principles into practice. It is not about tokenism or advantaging one group over another. It is about understanding the moral, ethical, legal and business benefits of implementing equality and inclusion policy and practices; recognising that, by doing so, we can gain the most for an organisation and the individuals within it, by not only valuing, but utilising the diversity of its people. Fairness is about equal treatment according to needs – the issue here is understanding what those needs are, based on the differences.

We see this as a highly effective way of ensuring that whole organisations have a consistent framework for looking at the intriguing world of differences and similarities; of assumptions about self and others; a world we all inhabit, yet about which we have, understandably, a myriad of views and assumptions.

We shall examine the various strands of diversity, and the link with inclusion and equality – or lack of it.

We're all diverse, and though some equalities legislation may have been started as a way to protect certain groups from discrimination, the law is written to protect us all. It is not about entitlement; it is about taking responsibility, firstly for your own assumptions and behaviours and focussing your thinking – are your values and beliefs helpful or unhelpful? Do they limit you and/or others?

It is said that there are three main cases for diversity, inclusion and equality

1. **Ethical/Moral** This is about doing something because it is right. There is a 'little voice' in us which checks on us to ensure we don't do wrong. If you treat an individual or group badly, simply because of some difference you see in them, that's discrimination; and for most of us, we'd know that it is wrong. You would feel it in your conscience, in the very pit of your stomach; it's simply not right, and you know it. We put this first, as it's simply about our humanity.

2. **Legal** Equalities legislation has developed over the years, as a response to some people treating unfairly others who are different to them, based simply on that difference. So, if you like, one reason for equality is that, if you treat people unequally, you break the law, and may end up in court. Tribunals are very costly, financially and emotionally, and can severely damage the reputation of an individual or organisation. It's the stick approach to equalities. It's a deterrent and punishment, but hardly the best reason for seeking a fair, just and equitable workplace/society.

    Most of us feel traffic lights are a reasonable method of ensuring vehicles pass through junctions safely and equitably, but some feel they shouldn't have changed just before them, so drive on, endangering others; thus, the need for cameras and fines.

3. **Business** There is a very strong business case for diversity, inclusion and equality. Put simply: if you only employ people who are like you – same accent, age, background, gender, ethnicity, etc – you are only drawing from a limited pool, and will struggle to compete with more diverse companies, who will have a wider range of ideas and abilities. By limiting your employee intake, you fail to reflect your potential clients/customers; so you are less likely to relate to them, and have them as clients/customers. An organisation which broadly selects

from its customers/clients, and is fair and just with all its employees, is the company most likely to progress in the long term and benefit commercially, thereby increasing productivity and profits. There are enormous economic advantages that can be enjoyed by companies, their clients, employees, stakeholders and suppliers, just by taking this path.

The financial cost of getting things wrong, wittingly or unwittingly, can result in payouts of thousands of pounds, apart from the emotional fallout, and the amount of time spent in recovery and repairing damaged reputation. Some employees, who experience indirect or direct discrimination, may leave and share their grievances with family/friends – clients / customers also do this. Others, who 'have to stay' within the organisation, might do so out of 'malicious obedience'. At work, they will do the bare minimum of what is required and will not go that extra mile when needed. The consequences are disgruntled individuals, lower productivity, and employees who can be perceived as difficult. The spiralling number of costly tribunal cases further highlights the need for organisations to focus on prevention and appropriate interventions.

Science Daily (3 April 2009)
Diversity Linked to Increased Sales Revenue and Profits,
More Customers
Workplace diversity is among the most important predictors of a business' sales revenue, customer numbers and profitability, according to research published in the April issue of American Sociological Review.

Gender diversity accounted for a difference of $599.1 million in average sales revenue. Those with lowest gender diversity averaged $45.2 million, compared to average sales of $644.3 million for businesses with most gender diversity.

Every percentage increase in rate of race or gender diversity equated to an increase in sales revenue of approximately 9% and 3% respectively.

Companies with highest gender diversity had on average 15,000 more customers than those with lowest.

Chapter Three

Responding to Difference

> *Difference is of the essence of humanity. Difference is an accident of birth and it should therefore never be the source of hatred or conflict. The answer to difference is to respect it. Therein lies a most fundamental principle of peace: respect for diversity.*
> John Hume

- **6 Types of Response**
- **Prejudice – Gordon Allport**
- **Types of Collusion**

Responding to Difference

The following is a list of ways that individuals and/or groups may well respond to someone who appears (skin colour, facial characteristics, dress) or sounds (accent, dialect, language intonation) different.

Six Responses to Difference

Xenophobia – Fear of another culture/lifestyle through hearsay or limited personal experience – can lead to hate.

Ethnocentrism – Feeling your culture/lifestyle is superior, to the detriment of others, leading to bigotry. Particularly likely in countries, to which people choose to migrate.

Forced Assimilation – The feeling that it is best all round if the newcomers take on all the aspects of the dominant culture, because, after all, it is superior and will serve them well.

Segregation – Belief that all communities are best served by staying separate, and being advised by their own cultural/religious leaders.

Acceptance – Belief that all cultures are equal, and therefore should be 'tolerated'. We have to get on with each other.

Celebration – Goes beyond tolerance, to positively praising the values of diversity, inclusion and equality, and what it has to offer. Unity is strength.

From Prejudice to Discrimination

We include this piece here, because its very premise is immutable, and can easily and regularly be related to issues from personal to global, from past to present, and, doubtless and sadly, to events still yet to come. Yet within it lie the very pointers as to how it can be avoided and limited in its influence. When responses to people, who are different in some way, revolve around xenophobia and ethnocentrism, then this model is most likely to occur.

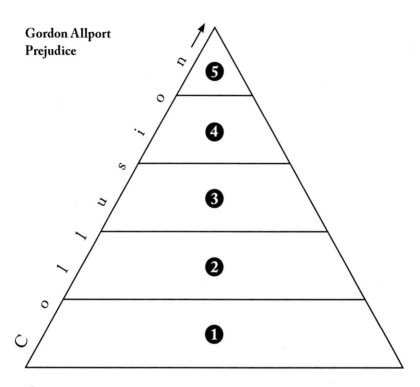

Gordon Allport Prejudice

Collusion

❶ Anti-locution

Most people who have prejudices talk about them with like-minded friends/ colleagues; occasionally, with strangers. They may express their contempt freely i.e. name-calling. People may never go beyond this level of dislike – can include ageist, racist, sexist, homophobic, religious jokes, which make assumptions and stereotype people and groups who are different.

- Exclusive behaviour, jokes and banter, name calling, unsavoury comments
- Inappropriate statements, assumptions, dismissing and minimising
- What could be added alongside is COLLUSION, for it is only by the silence of others that such villainy can prevail.

If you wish to bring down such a construction, the point of attack is at the bottom. At this level, far more people are involved, but at a stage which is not yet embedded. Do not ignore inappropriate comments/ humour, for doing so may be read as silent approval.

❷ Avoidance

If the prejudice is more intense, it leads the individual to avoid members of the disliked group, even perhaps at the considerable cost of inconvenience. Does not inflict physical harm on the group disliked, but may well cause considerable emotional/mental suffering to individuals or groups disliked.

❸ Discrimination

Here the prejudiced person makes detrimental distinctions of an active sort: undertaking to exclude all members of the group in question from certain types of educational opportunities, employment, residential housing or recreational privileges etc. Segregation is an institutionalised form of discrimination, enforced legally or by common custom.

❹ Physical/Mental/Emotional Attack

Under conditions of heightened emotion, prejudice may lead to acts of violence, or semi-violence, e.g. harassment, racial attacks or slogan daubing.

❺ Extermination/Genocide/Murder/Suicide

The ultimate degree of violent expression of prejudice. Suicide is included, to show the potential impact of constant bullying and discrimination, where the person or group stops just short of committing the final act, leaving that in the hands of the hapless 'victim'.

Types of Collusion

In a legal sense, collusion may be defined as a secret agreement or conspiracy for some fraudulent purpose. Yet, collusion is also a very natural human trait, when, as children, we learn to modify our behaviour, to fit in with expectations of parents, teachers, friends and society. In this way, we avoid being outsiders, and can feel accepted. But, as adults, we should be more able to make judgements about what is the right thing to do and avoid merely following the crowd in general, or caving in to the pressures to conform, exerted upon us by a few influential people.

The 3 forms of collusion are

1. **Silence** – the most common type; saying nothing, when others tell inappropriate jokes, behave badly to others or exclude them. People should feel empowered to 'rock the boat' and challenge appropriately.

2. **Denial** – assuming the ostrich position, so as to be able to claim that, 'We are all equal here'. You may blind yourself to obvious discrimination, simply because it's too painful to accept, or because you gain something by taking this stance.

3. **Active co-operation.** This could be laughing at inappropriate banter, or agreeing with discriminatory comments made by others, eventually becoming one of those who instigate such behaviour.

Chapter Four

Equalities Legislation

66 *Slowness to change usually means fear of the new.*
Philip Crosby

The Equality Act 2010
Rationale for 2010 Act
Getting Behind the Words

- **Harassment**
- **Victimisation**
- **Institutional Discrimination**
- **Discrimination: by association; by perception; direct; indirect; multiple discrimination; in-group discrimination**
- **Positive Action; Affirmative Action; Positive Discrimination**
- **A Racist Incident; Racism**
- **A Genuine Occupational Requirement (GOR)**
- **Stereotypes**
- **Archetypes**

Equalities Legislation
The Equality Act 2010 is intended to provide a new, cross-cutting, legislative framework, to protect the rights of individuals, and advance equality of opportunity for all; to update, simplify and strengthen the previous legislation; and to deliver a simple, modern and accessible framework of discrimination law which protects individuals from unfair treatment and promotes a fair and more equal society.

Rationale for 2010 Act
Previous laws developed over 40 years
- Nine major pieces of legislation;
- 100 statutory instruments;
- 2500 pages of guidance and codes of practice;
- Complex, difficult to understand;
- Streamline the law and produce a *single act* with plain explanations;
- Harmonisation of various concepts in equality.

The public sector Equality Duty came into force across Britain on 5 April 2011
Under the Equality Act 2010, there are nine protected characteristics or areas, where people are protected from discrimination. These nine characteristics are described in full later in *Chapter Five*.

For updated information
http://www.equalityhumanrights.com
http://www.homeoffice.gov.uk/equalities/equality-act/equality-duty

We have included the anti-discrimination legislation in *Chapter Fifteen*, because it has informed The Equality Act 2010, and will provide additional information with regard to diversity, inclusion and equality.

Getting Behind the Words

Harassment
A person engages in unwanted conduct, related to a relevant protected characteristic, and the conduct has the purpose or effect of violating another person's dignity or creating an intimidating, hostile, degrading, humiliating or offensive environment for another person.

Harassment also takes place if a person engages in unwanted conduct of a sexual nature, or that is related to gender reassignment or sex, and the conduct has the purpose or effect of violating another person's dignity, or creating an intimidating, hostile, degrading, humiliating or offensive environment for another person.

And, because of their rejection of or submission to the conduct, a person treats them less favourably than they would have treated them if the person had not rejected or submitted to the conduct.

Victimisation

With reference to equality, a person is victimised because another individual has contravened the Equality Act and they have given evidence or information about this. Giving false evidence or information, or making a false allegation, is not a protected act if the evidence or information is given, or the allegation is made, in bad faith. But, punishing or treating someone unfairly because they have made a complaint of discrimination, or are thought to have done so, or because they have supported someone else who has made a complaint of discrimination is also victimisation. Of course, victimisation, like harassment, occurs around any realm of unfairness.

Institutional Discrimination

This is the collective failure of an organisation to provide an appropriate and professional service to people because of their perceived difference, based on one or all of the protected characteristics. We would recommend that issues of accent, appearance, class, dialect, poverty, socioeconomics, etc are also included.

It can be seen or detected in processes, attitudes and behaviour which amount to discrimination through unwitting prejudice, ignorance, thoughtlessness and stereotyping which disadvantage/advantage individuals/groups.

Examples of Institutional Discrimination

1. Ineffective consultation and involvement;
2. Lack of information or communication;
3. Lack of monitoring and reviewing of policies and practices, and their impact on specific groups;
4. Lack of training and awareness;
5. Exclusion of specific individuals/groups from recruitment, retention and progression opportunities;

6. Marginalising employees;
7. Lack of support for employees;
8. Informal 'in groups' or cliques;
9. Assumptions and stereotyping;
10. Lack of openness to the personal values and beliefs of others;
11. Use of inappropriate language.

Discrimination by association – directly discriminating against someone because they associate with someone who has a protected characteristic.

E.g. somebody from a majority ethnicity receiving discrimination because they are going out with someone from a minority ethnicity.

Discrimination by perception – direct discrimination because it is believed that someone possesses a protected characteristic.

E.g. someone being discriminated against because people have decided that they are gay when they are not.

Direct Discrimination
A person discriminates against another person if, because of a protected characteristic, they treat them less favourably than they would treat others.

E.g. you continually manufacture reasons for not promoting a Black woman onto your all-White, male senior team, because it will, you feel, spoil your cozy little set-up: that she really isn't 'one of us'.

They do not discriminate against another person if they can show their treatment of another person to be a *proportionate* means of achieving a *legitimate aim*.

What is proportionate?
The employer has no reasonable alternative, other than to introduce, say, an age-based practice. For example, a construction firm hiring for physically demanding work that requires a good level of physical fitness; the employer might have a case for setting a maximum age for their on-site workers, for health and safety reasons. However, this also could be argued against, since an older person may be fitter than a younger person.

What is a legitimate aim?

A wide variety of aims may be considered legitimate, but they must correspond with a reasonable need for the employer. Economic factors, such as business needs and efficiency may be legitimate aims, but arguing that it could be more expensive not to discriminate will not be a valid justification.

Indirect Discrimination

A person discriminates against another if they apply a provision, criterion or practice which is discriminatory in relation to a relevant protected characteristic of another person; e.g. a lot of networking is carried out during lunchtimes in the local pub; although these are not official meetings, a lot of business is carried out, with those who attend gaining much benefit from this. This, however, indirectly discriminates against anyone whose religion prohibits their being in places where alcohol is served.

But not if a person can show it to be a proportionate means of achieving a legitimate aim.

In cases of discrimination, it is the impact, rather than the intention, which matters.

Other issues to consider regarding discrimination are as follows:

Multiple Discrimination

As a concept, multiple discrimination has emerged in academic and human rights forums to address the reality that experiences of discrimination are shaped by one's multiplicity of identity. As each individual has an age, a gender, a sexual orientation and an ethnicity, and some have or acquire a religion/belief or a disability, discrimination may be experienced on multiple grounds. For example, an individual belonging to a minority ethnic group may be a woman, a woman may be a lesbian, and a lesbian may be an individual with a disability.

In fact, one person could identify themselves or be perceived as all of these simultaneously and may experience specific and complex forms of discrimination on this basis. In recognising the complexity of identity, the concept of multiple discrimination endeavours to explain social realities, and shape approaches to addressing the complexity of discrimination, disadvantage and exclusion, in such a way as to better reflect these social realities.

January 2011. *Countryfile* presenter Miriam O'Reilly won her ageism case against the BBC. She didn't, however, win on the sexism aspect. It would seem that, while there clearly was ageism, in that a number of presenters had to make way for 'newer models' John Craven (68) was kept on, while three other women in their 40s were dismissed from the programme. In other words, there clearly appeared to be discrimination based additionally on their gender.

This is sadly quite a common case of multiple discrimination, where someone is treated negatively differently based on more than one aspect of their being, e.g. gender and race.

Nick Ross said he thought it was, "...undoubtedly tougher for women as they get older", but added that, "it might be easier for women – on looks – when they are younger, and I don't hear people complaining about that."

Good point, but it should not be about favouring at any stage, rather it being the best person for the job, i.e. based on ability, potential, skills, and – yes, personality and doubtless other factors – but please, please, please, no longer based on your age, looks, disability, sexual orientation etc.

In-group discrimination refers to a situation in which an individual is treated adversely, by his or her own community or reference group, on the basis of belonging to another vulnerable group. For example, a woman belonging to an ethnic minority may face racism from women belonging to the majority community. Conversely, this woman may also face discrimination from within her ethnic community, on the basis of her gender. This type of discrimination explains in part the increased frequency, intensity and specificity of experiences faced by victims of multiple discrimination, reinforcing their status as the most vulnerable. For the victim, in-group discrimination can be particularly damaging, as denial of equal treatment comes from a community which the victim wishes to relate to rather intimately, and from which the victim might need to seek support.

Thus, the fact that a particular group faces discrimination does not preclude the group or its members from exercising discriminatory behaviour. In-group discrimination can expose what has been referred to as the 'paradox of multicultural vulnerability': by remedying one type of vulnerability, multi-culturalist policies may reinforce other vulnerabilities.

For example, instances of in-group discrimination, such as early forced marriages, female genital mutilation and honour killings, have occurred in the name of culture. In the context of increasingly diversified societies, efforts to promote cultural respect must not allow cultural practices to override fundamental individual rights. At the same time, discussions of in-group discrimination must be treated in a sensitive manner, as they can too easily fuel opinionated sentiment, and support the tendency to 'blame the victim'. Indeed, for this reason, group members and victims alike may feel pressure to keep these practices hidden.

Positive Action

Since 1976, there has been much legislation outlawing discrimination in employment and in everyday life, around race and gender; and more recently in terms of sexual orientation, religion and belief, disability and age.

Definitions

So, let us examine the differences between positive action, affirmative action and positive discrimination.

Positive Action

Quite often, people get mixed up between positive action and positive discrimination; so let us clarify this, as follows:

Positive action is legal in this country, and is enshrined in legislation. Significantly, the dictionary definition is the most apt way of describing positive action.

- Positive - Helpful, providing encouragement.
- Action - Doing something.

Positive action happens in order to provide help to people from under-represented groups, who have traditionally suffered disadvantage. This is usually due to an inability to access services, education and societal benefits normally enjoyed by mainstream groups. It can take many forms; such as recruitment, or training programmes.

Positive Action is aimed at individuals/groups who:
- suffer a disadvantage connected to their protected characteristic;
- have different needs;
- are disproportionately low in representation;

Purpose of Positive Action

To create a more representative and diverse organisation, reflecting society
How can positive action achieve this?

Traditionally, due to disadvantages that people from minority groups have suffered, this often leads to levels of:
- Lack of self-esteem;
- Lack of self-confidence;
- Lack of self-reliance;
- Lack of opportunity;
- Lack of assertiveness;

Positive action initiatives aim to address these areas and anything else that prevents people from realising their full potential. The benefits are to the individual of course, but also to the organisation and society as a whole.

Positive Action allows a person or organisation to:
- Provide facilities to meet the needs of people from particular groups in relation to their training, education or welfare;
- Target job training at people from groups that are under-represented in a particular area of work, or encourage them to apply for such work.

Affirmative Action
This is currently being discussed and advocated by some groups. A pool of mainstream and minority candidates is identified as competent to be part of the organisation, and, when selection takes place, candidates are selected on the demographic requirements of the organisation. Preferred candidates are identified, so as to reflect the demographics of society.

Positive Discrimination
To treat one person or community more favourably than another, purely on the basis of historic disadvantage. For example, to select for employment a minority ethnic or female applicant, not because they were the best person for the job, but purely to address an existing employee imbalance.

This form of discrimination is not only unlawful, but also unethical. This is still illegal in Britain, due to the positive discriminatory element of selecting those preferred candidates, although it is used in other countries. Positive discrimination is *illegal* in this country, and advocates the selection of people on the basis of their protected characteristic.

A Racist Incident
"Any incident, which is perceived to be racist by the victim
or any other person"
Race Relations (Amendment) Act 2000.

Racism – The Race Relations (Amendment) Act 2000 states
"...that racism consists of conduct or words or practices, which
***disadvantage or advantage** people, because of their colour, culture, or*
ethnic origin. It can be subtle or overt, intentional or unwitting. It can be
personal – name-calling, abuse, harassment and violence."

*..*ism – The above definition can be extended to cover all aspects of*
discriminatory assumptions and behaviours, e.g.

...sexism consists of conduct or words or practices, which disadvantage or
advantage people because of their perceived difference. It can be subtle or
overt, intentional or unwitting. It can be personal – name-calling, abuse,
harassment and violence."

Not making reasonable adjustments
The Disability Discrimination Act requires employers to make
adjustments to working practices and environments, where necessary.
This is so that people with disabilities are not disadvantaged. Common
examples of workplace adjustments include:
* laying out furniture, so that a wheelchair user can move freely
  around the office;
* providing a toilet designed for disabled people;
* providing speech recognition software, to help someone with motor
  difficulties to use your I.T. systems.

A Genuine Occupational Requirement (GOR)
In some circumstances, an employer can make a case that a certain protected
characteristic needs to be considered a genuine occupational requirement, so
that they can advertise for someone with that characteristic.

E.g. A women's refuge could justifiably require a woman to work there,
as a man might well be deemed inappropriate.

Applicants may not agree that such a rule is appropriate or fair for a particular job. If so, they can still claim they have been unlawfully discriminated against. The employer would need to be able to explain and justify their particular situation.

Stereotypes

Stereotypes have three factors:
1. From an outsider's viewpoint
2. Restrictive or limiting
3. Accusative

i.e. someone observes behaviours from people from another culture/ethnicity/lifestyle. They then extend that to anyone from that culture. Banter, including racist/sexist/homophobic jokes and name-calling comes from this.

Archetypes

Archetypes are developed by people within that culture/lifestyle. They make general statements about the cultural values, norms and beliefs, without limiting anyone to them; they are informative, non-restrictive and often useful aids to better cross cultural relationships.

Chapter Five

Exploring the Nine Protected Characteristics
in the Equality Act 2010

❝❝ *Civilizations should be measured by the degree of
diversity attained and the degree of unity retained.*
Ola Joseph

1. **Age**
2. **Disability**
3. **Gender Reassignment**
4. **Marriage/Civil Partnership**
5. **Pregnancy and maternity**
6. **Race**
7. **Religion or Belief**
8. **Sex**
9. **Sexual Orientation – Bisexual; Gay; Heterosexual; Lesbian**

In law, there is no hierarchy within the following strands of diversity. However, it is quite common for people to think there is. Perhaps it is because some strands have been protected in law for longer and are therefore more ingrained in our awareness while others have been added more recently, with some people, (often those who believe that 'P.C. has gone mad') feeling, 'That's just taking it all too far'. For some, certain characteristics are more closely linked to themselves in some personal way, and, therefore, may be viewed as being much more serious. Not only that, but it is quite usual for those who face discrimination for a particular protected characteristic to be quite able to harass others, without seeing the ludicrousness of that.

People might say that calling a person or thing 'gay', is 'just a laugh', or, 'it's okay, we all joke around about age'; or, and it's well known, they will tell all and sundry that 'all 'Gippos' are thieves, and leave a mess everywhere'. People who might join in with, or even instigate such discrimination, would probably baulk at, say, racism or disablist comments. Yet, the truth is that they all do the same harm; cause the same pain. Indeed, I will add here that any discrimination, against any individual, causes them grief, whether the attack is against a protected characteristic or not.

Age – the one strand where we could all be discriminated.
It has, over generations, become standard practice to discriminate in the workplace around age; to accept it, indeed not even see it as discrimination; to assume you're not ready for certain positions, until you're of a 'mature' age; that, by a certain age, you're no longer fit for paid work; that, while you occupy the lower or upper levels of the age range, you will be fair game for receiving 'harmless jokes' about being 'still wet behind the ears' or 'drawing your pension'. Age discrimination legislation has come about to challenge this status quo in the realms of recruitment, employment and retirement. It aims for equality across the ages.

Ageism is still rife in the workplace, a YouGov survey has revealed. More than half (59%) of UK citizens aged over 55 have claimed that they see their age as being a 'major barrier' to current employment.

A Payroll World report also revealed that over two-thirds (70%) of over 55-year-olds are not confident of finding a job within three months of becoming unemployed. The report added that 84% of workers within the same age bracket would consider a different type of job from anything they have previously done, if they were made unemployed.

Unhelpful terms

mature for their age	girls/boys ('girls' can also be sexist, when used alongside men i.e. 'the girls will do this, while the men...')
old codger	we're looking for young, dynamic...
person with gravitas	having a senior moment
young pup	not out of nappies

Disability

Understanding the social model of disability is a critical factor in successfully meeting our duties under the Disability Discrimination Act.

> *'A social model approach states that people with impairments are disabled by physical and social barriers. The 'problem' of disability results from social structures and attitudes, rather than from a person's impairment or medical condition. This approach has influenced a rights-based view of equality for disabled people, and represents the key to understanding and implementing the Disability Equality Duty, the aim of which is to understand and dismantle the barriers which exclude and limit the life chances of disabled people.'*
> **Source: Disability Rights Commission Guidance**

An example of the social model in practice can be illustrated by a deaf person wanting to attend a conference. If no sign language interpreter is there, or induction loop for a hearing aid, the person is excluded – disabled. But, with a signer operating alongside the speakers, or an induction loop, the person can take part. They still have the same hearing impairment, but they are no longer disabled.

The social model asks what can be done *to remove the barriers to inclusion.*

In this approach, the disability is caused by the barrier, not the impairment.

Accessible buildings (with appropriate resources and support) and positive, aware and inclusive attitudes will not only be of benefit to the disabled members of the community, but also to disabled employees and the wider workforce who will benefit from the knowledge and experiences that their disabled colleagues bring.

Some Interesting Facts
- Only 17% of disabled people were born with their disability
- One in four people will be affected by mental ill health in the course of their life
- Mental health problems now account for more Incapacity Benefit claims than back pain
- Sickness absence cost the UK economy £16.8 billion in 2010
- Only 50% of disabled people of working age are in employment, compared to 80% of non-disabled people
- A third of those disabled people not working would like to work, compared to a quarter of non disabled people
- 70% of people with a disability, who are off work for a period exceeding 12 months, never return to work
  Source: The Shaw Trust

Language and terminology is, at times, historical, and words/rhymes or statements, once used, may now be seen as inappropriate and offensive.

Consideration should be given to words, which offend, patronise or minimise the individual's or group's identity, because of their perceived difference.

Often it is not the intent, but the impact that some words have on individuals/groups.

This is not intended to be an exhaustive list, nor a definitive guide, but a reminder of the impact that certain words may have.

Inappropriate	Appropriate
Handicap	Disability
Invalid	Disabled person
The disabled/The handicapped	Disabled people
Special needs	Additional needs
Patient	Person
Abnormal	Different or disabled

Victim of	Person who has/person with
Crippled by	Person who has/person with
Suffering from	Person who has/person with
Afflicted by	Person who has/person with
Wheelchair bound	Wheelchair user
The blind	Blind and partially sighted people or visually impaired people
The deaf	Deaf or hard of hearing people
Cripple or crippled	Disabled or mobility impaired person
The mentally handicapped	People/person with a learning difficulty or learning disability
Retarded/backward	Person with a learning disability
Mute or dumb	Person with (a) speech impairment
Mentally ill or mental patient	Mental health service user
Able bodied person	Non-disabled person

- Avoid using medical labels, as this may promote a view of disabled people as patients. It also implies the medical label is the over-riding characteristic; this is inappropriate;
- If it is necessary to refer to a condition, it is better to say, for example, 'a person with epilepsy' *not* 'an epileptic', or 'she/he has cerebral palsy' *not* 'a spastic';
- Avoid 'mental retardation/mentally retarded'.

Gender Reassignment

Gender Identity – Everyone has their own gender identity; this is simply whether a person feels like a man or a woman, combination of these or neither.

Gender Dysphoria – This is a medical term for the persistent discomfort and/or inability to live as a member of the gender a person was assigned to at birth.

Gender Reassignment Surgery – This is surgery to reconstruct secondary sex characteristics. The aim of these procedures is to make a person's gender identity and physical body congruent with each other, thereby reducing gender dysphoria. Surgeries differ between FTM (female to male) and MTF (male to female) individuals, and involve a number of procedures. Not all trans people undergo surgery, for a variety of social, medical and personal reasons.

If a person's gender presentation is at variance to the way they think about themselves, they may choose to pursue the possibility of surgical intervention or gender reassignment. 'Trans' is an umbrella term, to describe people whose gender identity is different from the sex they were assumed to be at birth. A person may have felt this disparity since childhood, growing up as a male, yet sensing they should be female, and vice versa.

Yet, also to be noted is that it is over simplification to see male and female as distinctly different entities; we are all made up of facets of each, and unthinkingly, unknowingly, will live quite happily with these. It is more useful to see gender identity as a spectrum running between female and male.

Gender Recognition Act (GRA) 2004
Legislation which gives transsexual people who have transitioned full legal rights as a member of the gender in which they are living, including the right to have their birth certificate revised.

Note that the above makes no mention of medical procedures – because that is not a requisite. Yet, a person deciding to live in the alternate gender would be covered by the Act. The terms 'trans woman' and 'trans man' indicate the gender of the person, as they now live. Sometimes, a person will simply say, "I'm trans".

During interviews and workshops, I have met parents who express concern over their child (usually male) for showing an interest in things they feel to be inappropriate to their gender. Traditionally, this tends to mean boys playing with dolls, or wanting to put on the girls' dressing up clothes in school. When asked, their anxiety is clearly about the boy being gay. Rarely, if ever, do they engage with the possibility of gender dysphoria. Transsexual and transgender are concepts many are ignorant of, and are generally beyond the realms of the imagination in children. Most parents/carers just accept it all as simple curiosity – a child trying to establish just exactly who they are; and this, generally will indeed be the case. We hear: 'It's just a phase'; 'They'll grow out of it', at times with the barely suppressed, 'Well, I sincerely hope so'.

Strictly for balance, it should be stated that some people take a different view of this, not believing there is sufficient, cast-iron, scientific proof of the very existence of gender dysphoria. Some feel this merely provides a convenient get-out clause for gay and lesbian people to avoid the often severe, even life-threatening discrimination, which, sadly, too many still face today. As an example, they cite Iran as having the highest level of state-provided transgender surgery. Is this because Iran is a particularly 'enlightened' country, with regard to gender reassignment, or is it rather hiding the existence of all but heterosexuality, and, as a by-product, allowing them to be 'accepted', by then having 'normal/valid' relationships with the opposite sex.

Transphobic Language
Language is, by its nature, living, mutable, and can then, at times, be unclear or contradictory. Thus, e.g. 'tranny' was previously used by some transgender people; then went out of usage, as it was readily used with ill intent by 'do-badders'; then, more recently, reclaimed by some trans people from the insult hurlers. Of course, this has also been done with 'poof', 'queer' and 'nigger'. Personally, I am never at ease with such insult reclamation, and regularly advise against it, feeling it to be far too dangerous, leading to copy-catting, and helping to extend the life of these abusive terms.

You may hear the term 'cis', as in 'cis people' – 'cisgender' is a synonym for non-trans people. It comes from the Latin 'cic', which means 'on the same side', and is used to describe someone who is comfortable in the gender they were assigned at birth.

Common ways people use to insult transgender people are:
- Keep getting your name wrong (i.e. using your previous one)
- Misgendering someone, i.e. he/she or his/her (lazy or deliberate?)
- There's the he/she/it
- Tranny boy!
- She-male
- Girl with a cock
- Dude with a vag

While presiding over her funeral, a pastor insulted a trans woman, who had been shot dead. He had basically indicated that God had let her get killed, so that others could be saved. Earlier, another cleric had stated that this was the consequence of living such a lifestyle. Around 100 of the 300 congregation walked out in protest.

A trans police officer was 'outed' by the press, with the headline 'Lady Boy in Blue'.

A son murdered his father, after finding out he was transsexual.

Terms to avoid

Sex Change
Individuals who are transitioning are validating their gender, not 'changing their sex'. Another offensive term is 'sex swap'

Tranny
This term may be used within the transgender community, but may well be seen as offensive when others use it (see previous comment).

Pre-op
This term may be seen as offensive, because it labels and simplifies a complex state of being.

Further Terminology for Clarification

Cross dresser
A person who chooses to wear clothing which is opposite to the gender they are assigned at birth. They may not choose to live constantly in this role, and do not question their gender identity. Sometimes, this word is preferred to being referred to as transvestite.

Drag Queen/King
An individual who is content with their gender, but, for the purpose of entertainment, wears the clothing of someone of the opposite gender to the one they were assigned at birth.

Intersex
A medical term, which includes a number of conditions, where there is uncertainty about the person's sex. At birth, there are times, when the sex of a baby may not be so clear; where internal organs, hormones and genitalia may give conflicting messages.

Marriage and Civil Partnership
It is illegal to discriminate against an employee who is married or in a

civil partnership. Additionally, both of these are to be treated in the same way, e.g. in the way of benefits.

The Civil Partnership Act of 2004 gave same sex couples similar responsibilities and rights as couples in a civil marriage. These cover such areas as inheritance tax, tenancy rights, pension benefits, social security, inter alia. Currently, however, civil partnerships are not permitted to take place in religious buildings, or have religious readings, symbols, or religious music; though, in Scotland, some churches offer religious blessings.

Additionally, to date, although we have civil partnership, UK law has not moved to same-sex marriage. For some same-sex couples, this feels like inequality – a discrimination of title, as well as, for some, the loss of a religious venue. Others, however, wish this distinction to remain, proud as they are of their sexual orientation; not wishing it to be hidden any more. Of course, it is this very aspect which is causing some issues, e.g. in monitoring forms, where some wouldn't want their status to be recorded as 'partner', as opposed to 'married', where 'partner' is the only option to single or divorced.

This strand is currently not covered in existing legislation (October 2011), with regard to:

Discrimination by association – directly discriminating against someone because they associate with someone who has a protected characteristic

Discrimination by perception – direct discrimination, because it is believed that someone possesses a protected characteristic

Indirect Discrimination – may occur when there is a rule applied to everyone, but negatively impacts on a particular protected characteristic

Harassment – employees can now complain about behaviour they find offensive, even if it's not directed at them

Harassment by a third party – employers could be held responsible for harassment of their staff, by someone they don't even employ

Pregnancy and Maternity

During pregnancy and any statutory leave, a woman has protection against discrimination on the grounds of her pregnancy and maternity. Any decision about employment must not take account of any absence for illness related to her pregnancy.

Pregnancy is the condition of being pregnant and expecting a baby.

Maternity relates to the period after birth, and is linked to maternity leave, if employed. Out of work, the period is 26 weeks for protection against maternity discrimination; this also includes treating a woman unfairly because she is breastfeeding.

Some examples of discrimination because of pregnancy or maternity leave:
- being dismissed because employer says they can't afford statutory maternity pay;
- being disciplined for underperforming because of an illness related to your pregnancy;
- being suspended for health and safety reasons and not receiving full pay;
- being suspended, dismissed or omitted from training courses because of your pregnancy/maternity;
- being chosen for redundancy, with pregnancy being given as a contributory reason;
- This strand is currently not covered in existing legislation (October 2011), with regard to:
- **Discrimination by association** – directly discriminating against someone because they associate with someone who has a protected characteristic
- **Discrimination by perception** – direct discrimination because it is believed that someone possesses a protected characteristic
- **Harassment** – employees can now complain about behaviour they find offensive, even if it's not directed at them
- **Harassment by a third party** – employers could be held responsible for harassment of their staff by someone they don't even employ

Race and ethnicity

For the most part, people view both these terms as similar, if not the same. If you are discriminated against, it matters little whether it is for your ethnicity or race. Race can be associated with biology or nature, ethnicity with culture or nurture. Your ethnicity you may view as British, but your ethnic origin or race may be Asian. Ethnicity has more personal choice about it; race you are labelled with – you can't decide to be of a certain race; but you take on the language, the literature, the culture, customs and practices of an ethnicity, and can choose to become that or not – even though some people will still never view you as belonging to what they see as their select group/ethnicity.

When I have interviewed people (even adults), they may not know the word ethnicity, let alone have an idea what theirs is. Often, they will say, "Well, I suppose I am (e.g.) Bangladeshi". When I ask them, if that is what they feel or want, they may say, "Actually, I was born here; never been to Bangladesh, and I just feel British."

Race is much more of an imposed, 'pseudo-scientific' social construct, which once was Black or White, but continues to change, now including South Asian, South East Asian, etc. It tends to create a hierarchy of the advantaged and disadvantaged, and was a predominant factor at the height of the slave trade.

I define myself as British born and also Chinese and Russian, and at other times may say I am a Londoner.

'Colour of Skin' is an obvious difference/similarity in appearance – issues raised could be around lighter or darker skin colour

Why focus on these aspects?
Race, ethnicity, and colour of skin have ramifications for assumptions, prejudice and stereotypes, both positive and negative. Negative assumptions and prejudice are also not limited to race or only skin colour – they cover, for example, anti-Semitism, discrimination and prejudice towards Travellers and Roma Gypsies. However, a person's race and ethnicity, together with the colour of their skin, accent and language are an immediate indication that someone may be different or the same; but it may be in those aspects alone. Judgements, as well as negative attitudes, can be made without sufficient knowledge, just based on the individual's race, ethnicity, and colour of skin.

> *"It never ceases to amaze me that men (sic) should feel honoured by the humiliation of their fellow human beings."*
> ***Mahatma Ghandi***

Prejudice

It is an evident global factor that societies habitually treat people differently, based on many factors. A major one is that of race, ethnicity and colour of skin. The dominant group will tend to treat other ethnicities as inferior. For 'White' societies, 'Black' skin may have many negative facets, in addition to the basic prejudices. In 'Black' societies, the skin tone may well have a bearing on how a person is viewed.

For England, racism is wide ranging, and within it has a hierarchy; there have been long-held historical prejudices against the other parts that make up the less than aptly named United Kingdom, holding aspects of Irish, Welsh and Scottish culture to be intellectually 'inferior'. Equally, if an English person were to visit Ireland, Wales or Scotland, they too may experience racism. In Europe, past wars have left a legacy of distaste and xenophobia for the French and the Germans.

We need also to highlight the prejudice that Travellers and Gypsies within our society experience, because of their chosen lifestyles, and to acknowledge that anti-Semitism is prevalent within our society. Equally, the effects of war and civil unrest within countries will usually lead to a larger movement of people around the world, and countries where they tend to go are likely to see a rise in hatred and discrimination towards Asylum Seekers and Refugees. Our views are fuelled with fear and ignorance, and can be strengthened by the negative influence of family, peers and the media, unless positive action is taken to counterbalance these views.

"If you know nothing about a person, you can believe anything"
Dervla Murphy

I have included the following report, because this case was instrumental in the **Race Relations (Amendment) Act 2000**, which came about as a result of the commitment and dedication of Doreen and Neville Lawrence, the parents of Stephen Lawrence.

Stephen Lawrence Inquiry Report

On 22 April 1993, Black 18-year-old Stephen Lawrence was murdered by a group of five or six White youths in Eltham, South East London.

In July, charges against two youths were dropped. The Crown Prosecution Service said there was insufficient evidence to continue with the prosecution. A private case was launched by the Lawrence family in April 1994 but it collapsed two years later – identification evidence relating to three youths was ruled inadmissible, leading to acquittal.

In March 1997, the Police Complaints Authority (PCA) announced it would carry out an investigation into the case. In July of that year, then Home Secretary Jack Straw announced an inquiry into Stephen's death, to be chaired by Sir William Macpherson.

Sir William said the inquiry was a response to "explicit complaints and serious unease about the conduct by individual officers and the Metropolitan Police Service (MPS), in their investigation of Stephen Lawrence's murder."

The investigation was marred by a combination of professional incompetence, institutional racism, and a failure of leadership by senior officers.

Opening with some background details of social developments in the 1970s and 1980s, the report made links between these factors and the culture which developed within the police service, painting a negative picture of officers who were indifferent, abrasive and of a low standard, many of whom are still currently serving.

The report highlighted the dangers of reactive, fire-brigade policing, and the gap this creates between officers and their communities.

Black people felt over-policed as crime suspects and under-protected as crime victims – fuelled by their perception of stop and search, use of CS spray and deaths in police custody.

Police perspective: morale very low, and unwillingness to consider public's perspective. Felt their concerns were over-stated; that stop and search was valuable and justifiable for their role. Unwillingness, by both sides, to see the others' point of view.

Race/Ethnicity – Inappropriate and Appropriate Language
Consideration should be given to those words which offend, patronise or minimise the individual's or group's identity, because of their perceived difference.

Often, it is not the intent, but the impact that some words have on individuals/groups.

This is not intended to be an exhaustive list, or a definitive guide, but as a reminder of the impact that certain words may have.

Language may change, and, at the time, seem appropriate; but consideration needs to be given to the following examples:

Inappropriate	Appropriate
Coloured	Black
Half-caste	Dual Heritage – Diverse Heritage – mixed race is commonly used but can have a sense of being mixed up and less than, and is therefore not my preferred term
Red Indians	Native Americans
Third World Developing Country	Specify the name of the country (scientific, artistic, cultural and technological achievements are not exclusively Western or European)
Black day	A bad day or a memorably sad day
Afro-Caribbean	African or African-Caribbean, (avoid Afro, which refers to a hair style)

During a workshop recently I was asked, 'Is it true that Black people can't be racist?' I was surprised about this question, (anyone can be racist) because I had not heard this comment for many years – at least since the Race Relations (Amendment) Act 2000, when the definition of a racist incident and racism was clarified.

'A racist incident is any incident perceived to be racist by victim or another person'.

The incident may or may not be racist – however the organisation has a duty to prevent all forms of racism/discrimination, and should have learning and development courses in place to ensure that there is no institutional discrimination (witting or unwitting), as well as procedures to log, record and investigate any allegations of unfair treatment. The Chief Executive, Senior Leadership Team, Chair and Leader of Council have the vicarious liability to prevent all forms of discrimination, and

I would recommend that all employees have induction/training on understanding diversity, inclusion and equality and their personal responsibilities. Racism can advantage or disadvantage someone because of their race – there can be a danger that an individual is promoted beyond their current abilities and/or not promoted because of the assumptions made, based on their race/ethnicity. Similarly, this definition can be used for all the protected characteristics i.e. a man who works in a non-traditional occupation, such as nursery teaching, may well be advantaged or disadvantaged based on the assumptions made by the decision makers. The list of examples could be endless.

However, the fear of being called a racist may well have led to a fear of doing the wrong thing, and/or confusion about what you should or shouldn't say. To further exemplify this confusion, I was told that a participant was queuing for refreshments, and, when asking for a black coffee, was told by another colleague that they should not say this, because it was inappropriate. Much confusion and even conflict may occur because we hold on to opinions or views which are not valid, or are unhelpful myths.

Religion or Belief

The law defines this as any religion – major or less widely practised – and any religious or philosophical belief (not political). You are also protected in the law from discrimination for not having a religion or belief. You are not obliged to tell an employer of your religion or belief, though that would help them offer any facilities, if so required. The employer, however, is not obliged to offer facilities (e.g. prayer/quiet room), nor time off for religious reasons – though to do so would be good practice, where possible. Where a religion requires certain types of clothing, a flexible clothing policy will usually avoid any conflict, unless to do so contravenes health and safety policies.

It is illegal to refuse to offer services to certain people because of their religion or belief, (or lack of). However, certain religious organisations may be allowed to discriminate against people of another religion/belief, e.g. faith schools. The organisation must be non-profit making, and the discrimination deemed necessary, to meet their religious aims, or to avoid offending those who share those aims. Charities too may be allowed to provide their services and benefits only to people of a certain religion or belief, so long as that is stipulated in its constitution.

This particular protected characteristic tends to find itself at odds with some other protected characteristics, in particular sexual orientation, as can be seen in the case studies provided in this book. The conflict comes about where a person interprets their religion as indicating that anything other than heterosexuality is wrong, and they refuse to carry out an aspect of their job, or otherwise treat gay, lesbian or bisexual people in a discriminating manner. Generally, the ruling in such cases comes down to the fact that their belief does not allow them to discriminate against other protected groups. Basically, the laws of a country take precedence over a person's religion or belief.

The Employment Equality (Religion or Belief) Regulations came into force on 2 December 2003. These regulations made it unlawful for employers to discriminate on the grounds of religion or belief.

Employers should ensure they have policies in place which are designed to prevent discrimination in:
recruitment and selection;

- determining pay;
- training and development;
- selection for promotion;
- discipline and grievances;
- prevention of bullying and harassment.

Definitions
'Religion' means any religion, and a reference to religion includes a reference to a lack of religion.

'Belief' means any religious or philosophical belief, including a reference to a lack of belief.

A reference to religion includes a reference to lack of religion, and a reference to belief includes a reference to lack of a belief.

Everyone has the right to freedom of thought, conscience and religion; this right includes freedom to change his/her religion or belief, and freedom, either alone or in community with others, and in public or private, to manifest her/his religion or belief, in worship, teaching, practice and observance.

Freedom to manifest one's religion or belief shall be subject only to such limitations as are prescribed by law and are necessary in a democratic society in the interests of public safety for the protection of public order, health or morals, or for the protection of the rights and freedoms of others.

In the UK, Muslims form the largest group belonging to a non-Christian religion, and have the lowest employment rates of all religious groups.

Most religiously motivated hate crimes are acts of vandalism, although personal attacks are not uncommon. Following the terrorist attacks of 9/11 and 7/7, there was a specific rise in Islamophobia, with Muslim women having their hijab snatched off their head, along with other abuse – clear, direct discrimination.

An example of indirect discrimination is, when you conduct not just social gatherings, but even business meetings, in the local pub. This is likely to make it difficult for anyone whose religion prohibits alcohol, or places where it is consumed. Whether unthinking or deliberate, such decisions can lead to exclusion and probable unfairness at work, around environment, non-inclusive culture, and opportunities for promotion.

Sex Discrimination
Sex discrimination was the first of the protected characteristics to have a Commission, whose work focussed on the rights of women and men – The Equal Opportunities Commission 1975, followed by The Commission for Race Equality 1979, and the Disability Rights Commission 1999. These Commissions merged into the Equality & Human Rights Commission in 2007.

Girls and boys are treated differently from birth, and may well be socialised by experiencing different language, dress, play, expectations and behaviours. This affects the learning process. Before girls and boys leave nursery, stereotyped notions of 'masculinity' and 'femininity' are already absorbed.

The popular view of 'masculinity' is toughness, dominance, independence, eagerness to fight and repression of empathy. The corresponding view of females is that they are weak, non-aggressive, kind, caring and passive. All these descriptions are mediated by cultural practices, customs, traditions, race, religion or beliefs, and social class.

The socialisation and media concept of boys has increasingly encouraged the above concept of masculinity – instead of moving away from it – as indeed has the concept of what girls should be like.

Women, as a whole, are not passive, unselfish and unsure, just as men, as a whole, are not active, ambitious and aggressive. Individual men and women vary greatly in their characteristics and behaviours. Gender stereotyping is dangerous, as it limits life expectations and experiences for boys/men and girls/women, as we internalise the myths to a greater or lesser degree.

Sexist Language carries negative assumptions about girls and women, boys and men, and can affect individuals' self-worth and confidence. Sexist language is dangerous, and both pervasive and widespread.

It is unacceptable, because it:
- Reinforces stereotypes by gender;
- Assumes the 'normal' terms of reference are male (e.g. using 'he' when referring to both women and men);
- Can be used to humiliate, put down and harass women and men. Psychologically and emotionally both women and men will be affected;
- Leads to a culture that condones different forms of violence against women, including domestic violence;
- Restricts men and women from acting in ways which are not traditionally masculine/feminine;
- Can lead to violence, which may be linked to learned 'macho' behaviour;
- Impacts on the way men and women behave, and hence their career pathways and/or job specialities.

'He/Man' Language
Do not use 'man' to mean humanity in general. There are alternatives: Sexist – man /mankind, Non-sexist – person, people, human-beings, men and women, humanity, humankind.

When reference to both sexes is intended, a large number of phrases use the word man or other masculine equivalents e.g. 'father' ('forefathers'), and a large number of nouns use the suffix 'man', thereby excluding women from the picture we present of the world. These should be replaced by more precise, non-sexist alternatives, as listed below:

Language and the British Sociological Association: Sex and Gender
The BSA grants free non-commercial use and non-commercial photocopying rights of these guidelines to promote good practice; we ask that you acknowledge the BSA, if you publish them.

Sexist/Exclusive	More acceptable/inclusive
man on the street, layman	people in general, people, lay person, non-expert
man-made	synthetic, artificial, manufactured
the rights of man	people's/citizens' rights; the rights of the individual
chairman	chair
foreman	supervisor
manpower	workforce employees, labour force, employees
craftsman/men	craftsperson/people
manning the reception	staffing the reception
to a man	everyone, unanimously, without exception
man hours	work hours
the working man	worker, working people
one man show	one person show
policeman/fireman	police officer/fire-fighter
forefathers	ancestors
founding fathers	founders
old masters	classic art/artists
masterful	very skillful
master copy	top copy/original
Dear Sir/s	Dear Sir/Madam

I have heard a number of common expressions which are non-affirmative and unacceptable, and are often used, across the protected characteristics, as forms of intimidation and bullying:

'the weaker sex'; 'big girl's blouse'; 'dumb blondes'; 'the little woman'; 'her indoors'; 'a bit of stuff'; 'boys don't cry'; 'boys will be boys'; 'queer'; 'fatty'; 'mental'; 'thick'; 'dumb'; 'head case'; 'mong'; 'frog'; 'yid'; 'gippo'; 'idiot'; 'paddy'; 'paki'; 'four-eyes', 'gay', 'ginger' etc.

These expressions may be used wittingly or unwittingly; either way, they can have a long-term negative impact on the individual and/or the group they are attacking (including indeed the users themselves).

Inclusive words are: we, people, everyone, you, etc.

Words with positive and negative connotations
The words 'boys' and 'gentlemen' are rarely used to refer to men in written work or speech. Nevertheless, women continue to be referred to or spoken to as if they were a 'breed apart', e.g., 'mere women' 'ladies' and/or 'girls', as if they had not yet reached adulthood. So, don't use 'boys' or 'girls', if that is age inappropriate; and don't use 'girls' where you wouldn't also refer to the males as 'boys'.

The use of such terms is often patronising and offensive, and should be avoided. In written work, it is inaccurate to write 'young girls' when referring to teenage young women. In speech, terms like 'love' and 'dear' also frequently can cause offence, especially when used in a patronising tone/manner, and should generally be avoided, though you can probably think of situations where no offence is meant, and none taken, especially when used to both sexes equally. So, "Would you like brown or white toast with that, love?" is something I positively cherish; whereas, "The steering wheel is the big, round thing, in front of you, dear" is the sort of comment we could all do without, thank you very much.

It is important to remember that, whilst many of the words used to describe men are positive, words used to describe women often have (some) negative connotations. Examples here include bachelor (free and easy) and spinster (sad and lonely); sir (respect) and madam (a right little madam). Some of the worst insults directed towards men make reference to women (e.g. 'old woman', 'son-of-a-bitch') and some of the most offensive (directed at women and men) refer to women's genitalia, where being called that is generally regarded, interestingly, as worse than the male sex organ.

Choice words
A multinational company was concerned that only 5% of applications in Europe came from women. It assumed that its technical, sales-oriented business did not appeal to them. Its recruitment advertising showed a young businessman with a dark suit and briefcase, and the text spoke of the need for aggression, dynamism and competitiveness. The company

decided to change the ad, featuring its own senior women instead. The text contained messages about enthusiasm, innovation and audacity. The application rate from women jumped to 40%.

During a very interesting seminar I attended at Kings Place London – University of Cambridge Centre for Gender Studies (in association with the *Guardian*) 16 November 2010, with Professor Deborah Cameron, of the University of Oxford presenting, her focus was 'What is the relationship to language and gender?'

She raised some of the following issues:
- *The amount women and men talk is not based on research evidence, but more on generalisations and folklore*
- *There are no significant gender differences in the amount women and men talk informally;*
- *Formally, men talk more than women – this is not about gender difference, but more about status;*
- *It is not how you speak, but how you are heard;*
- *No universal patterns of gender difference in behaviour;*
- *Peers influence you more than your family;*
- *Women have more personally at stake about what this means.*

Sexuality and Sexual Orientation are far too often used as if they are one and the same; yet they are not simply synonyms, however closely related they may seem. The issue is that sexuality is far too frequently used, where sexual orientation is what is meant – rarely, if ever, the other way round.

So, briefly, this is what the terms mean.

Sexuality is how people experience their own unique sexual life or sexual self and express themselves as sexual beings. It's about physicality and emotions; what we do and how we feel. It's the sexual point to our character, if you like.

Sexual Orientation is a person's sexual or emotional attraction to the opposite sex, same sex or both sexes.
- bisexual – attraction to men and women
- heterosexual – attraction to the opposite sex
- homosexual* – attraction to the same sex

It can be seen how sexuality and sexual orientation have clearly defined differences; so, let's use the correct term. Generally, it is people who are not heterosexual who will receive discrimination for their sexual orientation. An individual's sexuality is a different matter, and rarely comes under attack.

Homophobic attitudes and behaviour
Homophobic abuse is endemic in society, with 'gay' now the most common put-down. Unchallenged, homophobic language is so ingrained in everyday language that even the word 'gay' has been appropriated to mean anything worthless, poor quality or broken.

Individuals may also experience indirect homophobic abuse, not directed towards a particular person or group, but used when remarks are made to pass negative judgement, such as 'your bag is so gay' or 'that ring tone is gay'.

Is offensive language, such as gay, poof and queer, challenged? If not, your silence is taken as implicit approval (see collusion).

The term homosexual is clearly a correct term, and linguistically the opposite of heterosexual. However, it may be used negatively, at times, as if 'homosexuality' were a scientific abnormality or pathology. Therefore, people in (but not exclusively) the LGB communities prefer the terms gay man, lesbian (gay is still prevalent as a general term to cover gay men and women) and bisexual.

Chapter Six

Not in the Nine Protected Characteristics, but equally important

> *Our object in the construction of the state is the greatest happiness of the whole, and not that of any one class.*
> Plato

- **Socioeconomics – Class – Poverty**

People's characters may be judged on how much or how little money they have, which may then go on to provide access, or erect barriers, to many areas of their lives: health, justice and education being three major ones. There is, however, a necessity to have a shared understanding and awareness about the effects that socioeconomics, class, poverty and unemployment can have upon the lives of all people.

As with all aspects of diversity and equality of opportunity, caution needs to be taken about stereotyping an individual or a group because of their perceived identity. However, the effects of socioeconomics, class and poverty need to be acknowledged, and the following definitions may help clarify the issues raised for ensuring fairness and equitability for everyone.

Socioeconomics – refers to placing individuals into social groups, according to their financial status, and is often used instead of class in order to categorise people, who may move from one 'inherited' group to another, with the additional benefits that money may provide them i.e. home ownership and holidays several times a year in different countries.

Class – is viewed as a combination of money, birth heritage, profession, language and accent. Class identity can most simply be understood, in terms of past and present conditions. On the one hand, we have the experiences of our whole childhood. This is then overlaid by formal education, employment and lifestyle of adulthood. Therefore, defining people as belonging to a particular class is often problematic, as they may fulfil the criteria of more than one class.

Poverty – while lack of money is its most evident manifestation, there is additionally a poverty of care, love and attention; a poverty of positive experience, both of which may be prevalent in families of any income bracket.

One of the difficulties in focussing on these areas (hence why so often they are ignored) is that the images that prevail may be interpreted as a hierarchy of values and beliefs, i.e. poverty, class, socioeconomics equate with being in superior or inferior positions. More important is the recognition that individuals are diverse, and hence are affected differently by the circumstances in which they live.

Chapter Seven

The financial costs of discrimination Cost, **Cost, COST.**

> *One day, our descendants will think it incredible that we paid so much attention to things like the amount of melanin in our skin or the shape of our eyes or our gender, instead of the unique identities of each of us as complex human beings.*
> Franklin Thomas

There now follows employment tribunal cases where there have been considerable financial pay outs. However, I have chosen not to name the organisation, or indeed the individuals. Yearly, British businesses lose around £26 billion in sickness absence and lost productivity, or £1,035 per employee. However, with greater awareness and mental health support, businesses could save one third of these costs – a mammoth £8 billion a year.

16th May 2011, **Mind** found appalling attitudes towards mental ill health at work.

Age discrimination alone costs the economy £31 billion every year.

The National Audit Office estimates that the overall cost to the economy from failure to fully use the talents of people from ethnic minorities could be around £8.6 billion annually.

Case Studies – the costs of discrimination
In 2007, employers paid out around £4 million in compensation for discrimination cases; in 2009, it was almost £8 million. Across the protected characteristics, the average award was almost £21,000.

Age – A woman in her fifties, a few years from retirement, was passed over for promotion, in favour of a much less experienced person. A tribunal found there was no other possible explanation, in this case, than discrimination on the grounds of age. She was awarded more than £180,000.

An employment appeal tribunal found a woman guilty of making 'vexatious claims'. She had applied for a number of newly qualified posts, even though she was long qualified in the industry. If she were not offered the job, she would claim age discrimination, and gained many thousands of pounds by settling out of court. Her claim that she had only been trying to highlight the issue of age discrimination was dismissed, when it was discovered that she had refused any of the jobs she had been offered.

Disability – An employee suffering post traumatic stress disorder, following an assault at work, found they were no longer able to carry out their customer-facing role. They applied for a position taking phone calls, but were overlooked in favour of a non-disabled person. The company was found to have failed to make reasonable adjustments – the award was £80,000.

A landmark case was won at The Court of Appeal, when a company wrongfully withdrew a job offer to a person suffering from osteoarthritis. Their reason was that they felt he would not be able to carry the kit required to act as a rep (brought in since the original job offer), despite him offering suggestions as to how this could all be managed. Its significance is the difficulty of proving discrimination at recruitment, especially with arthritis.

A woman won a case of discrimination by association. Her child was born with disabilities, which required her to ask for more flexible working conditions, such as were readily granted to colleagues for other reasons. Instead, she was harassed, and required to work her normal hours.

Gender Reassignment – A trucker won a tribunal, following abuse, attacks and job discrimination. This followed her coming to work as a woman, not as her workmates had previously known her.

A tribunal judged that an organisation discriminated against a woman. They had offered her a job, and then withdrawn it, on being told the former special forces commander was transgender.

Marriage & Civil Partnership – A gay couple were found to have been discriminated against for their sexual orientation, and were awarded £1,800 each. The Christian hoteliers said they had refused to allow them to stay, as they would anyone, because of their belief in no sex outside of marriage. But, since the men were a couple in a civil partnership, the court found that they had illegally discriminated against the men on the basis of their sexual orientation, and, for all intents and purposes, against the state of civil partnership.

Maternity & Pregnancy – In 2010, an employee received 'a considerable settlement' after suffering insensitive comments and unfair treatment following a still birth. This was further exacerbated by receiving treatment far inferior to that of her female colleagues, during her next maternity leave, the following year.

In 2009/10, in Northern Ireland, two women got reimbursement of £8,000. One had been offered completely inappropriate hours to fit child minding arrangements. The other woman had it written into her contract that she could act up, in her manager's absence. However, she was informed, on returning from maternity leave, that she could not do that, as she would not know what she was doing.

Race – A Malaysian man was found to have suffered racial discrimination, after seeking help from the Equalities Commission to challenge what he believed to be unfair treatment over holidays and redundancy. The company failed to produce any equality policy in their defence, or any evidence of any equalities training.

An employment tribunal found that a bank had discriminated against an employee on the basis of his skin colour, ethnic origin or nationality, when they made him redundant. The tribunal made reference to the lack of equalities training for middle and senior management, the unfair redundancy process, and their specific victimisation of the claimant, in making the award of £2,800,000 (challenged on basis that he may well have left anyway).

A senior nursing boss was awarded £115,000 for racial discrimination, after being told, when asking about promotion, that she was, "the wrong colour and wrong culture". Previously, she had been left to work in her car, while White colleagues occupied desk space.

Religion or Belief – In 2008, a registrar was threatened with the sack, for refusing, due to her beliefs, to officiate in Civil Partnerships. Following her receiving bad treatment at work, and the fact that the council did not need her to work in these ceremonies, the court found in her favour. However, an employment appeal tribunal overturned this, confirming that it is illegal to refuse a service to someone based on their sexual orientation. She was refused permission to take this to the Supreme Court. The European Court of Human Rights states that employees do not have "an unqualified right to manifest their religion". Indeed, the registrar's issue had not been that she was being treated differently, but that she wasn't, and felt she should be. The council's policy, in fact, clearly included not permitting discrimination on the grounds of religion or belief.

Both the previous and following cases could well have been included in the sexual orientation section.

In 2010, a counsellor lost their appeal for wrongful dismissal. They had refused, on religious grounds, to work with same-sex couples. However, they had signed up to the organisation's equality policy, and thus were found to have breached the terms of their employment, and to have illegally discriminated.

A tribunal found in favour of the claimant for unfair dismissal, on the grounds of religious discrimination. A Christian charity that had previously employed non-Christian staff now wanted only to employ Christian staff, and was not going to offer promotion to its non-Christian staff. This was not viewed as a case of Genuine Occupational Requirement, and so the charity was found guilty of religious discrimination.

Sex – A male lawyer was awarded £123,000 damages when it was ruled that his company had sexually discriminated against him. He and a woman colleague were both being considered for redundancy. They were assessed to see which one would be kept on. On one of the criteria, the woman was scored 100%, which was the company's norm for women on maternity leave (they say to avoid their being disadvantaged). The employment tribunal said this effectively and unfairly tipped the balance in favour of the woman, in this rare occurrence of a man even claiming, let alone winning, a case of sex discrimination.

An American company was hit for $250 million in a sex discrimination class action case. Women were, on average, earning around $105 per month less than their male counterparts. Additionally, one area of their operations was described as being run like a boys' club, where one particularly unsavoury manager had shown some internet porn to a female colleague. On reporting this matter, she was told he couldn't really be sacked for that, as it wasn't actual violence towards her. It took two years before he was finally dismissed.

A woman truck driver won a sex discrimination case. Having worked successfully for the firm, as a long-distance driver, she applied to be an in-town pickup driver. They refused a number of her applications, stating that women were accident prone, and giving the jobs to less-experienced men. Eventually, they relented, and all was well for a long time, until she injured an ankle at work. On return, she was asked to carry out a physical test, which was not generally required for all workers, and which she failed. She was dismissed, and so brought a case of sex discrimination. It was found against the company, in that they had clearly not wanted to have women doing this particular job, and had required the test simply as a way to sack her.

Sexual Orientation – A man quit his job, after suffering taunts and sexual innuendo about his sexual orientation. The man, heterosexual, married, with children, was harassed by four colleagues who were fully aware of this, yet persisted in this inappropriate behaviour. The judge decided that he had indeed suffered discrimination, based on his sexual orientation, whatever that is, and whether or not the offenders were aware of it or not.

A gay man won £50,000 compensation when a court decided he had been discriminated against for his sexual orientation. The youth worker had received praise for his work in other dioceses, but this particular bishop probed him during the interview with questions about his sexual orientation before 'phoning him later to inform him he had not got the job.' The diocese stated that it was really to do with the church's position that sexual relations should only take place within marriage; that it would be the same situation, whatever the candidate's sexual orientation – the court found differently.

Chapter Eight

'The way we do things around here'

❝ *Assumptions are the termites of relationships.*
Henry Winkler

- **Unwritten Rules**
- **Values and Beliefs, based on diverse experiences**
- **The socialisation process**
- **Assumptions – Behaviour – Outcomes**

Unwritten rules are the rules which dictate how things are 'really done around here'. They are unhelpful aspects of organisational culture, and can often compete with individuals feeling that the organisation's diversity, equality or inclusion policy is actually being carried out.

When we join a new team, department or organisation, we learn very quickly what these rules are. Regardless of organisational policies, processes, structures and values, we soon find out how it is we are expected to behave in order to fit in, get along with others, gain promotion, or even just to survive. *"More than my job's worth to confront someone about their inappropriate use of language or behaviour, especially if they are senior to me."*

Quite often, these 'unwritten rules' will be at odds with our own values and those of the organisation. Our behaviour may then feel at odds with our values. This tension can create dissatisfaction within us, and can impact on our overall performance and how we feel about working with the organisation.

Sometimes, we unwittingly perpetuate the 'unwritten rules', and so establish an environment that does not support our teams to be the best they can be. At other times, we may feel we have to compromise our own values, in order to fit in or get on, which can lead to some people leaving the organisation, and others never truly achieving their potential. We influence the behaviour of others through our own behaviour. Hence, it is vital that the commitment to diversity, inclusion and equality is understood and demonstrated by the top team, board members and all employees.

Values and Beliefs – based on diverse experiences

To value something is to place importance on it. Values are those things that are important to us. They permeate most of what we do, and they are the key to what we do and why we do it.

This varied hierarchy of values can illustrate how people's priorities may seem strange from culture to culture, causing misunderstanding between people who hold different values; e.g. some cultures place more value than others on families staying together, living with each other and forming extended families.

Beliefs can change according to personal and professional experiences – they may change slowly or rapidly, dependent upon the individual's knowledge and skills in being able to take on new and/or conflicting information. Further key issues will be the beliefs inherited from within your own family, and from friends, teachers, religious leaders, the media etc. I have been at workshops where participants have asked me *"How do I deal with a family member, who is racist and says the most appalling things"* or *"I haven't seen my family for years, because they could not accept that I am gay."* I have heard some very sad things about how unkind people can be to others, based on their values, and believing they are right and others are wrong.

Values and beliefs can change life situations – *how* we think can create barriers, as much as *what* we think. To know how best to communicate, one needs to know how a person thinks. Values and beliefs can change with experience and with specific events that have an impact on our thoughts and feelings, such as bereavement, ill health etc. A change in the way we think and feel about something can also be positive, such as birth, change of environment, change of job, personal and professional achievements or change of circumstances. A lot will depend upon the individual's sense of self-worth, identity and confidence, as well as their ability to forgive themselves and others.

Behaviour

Our behaviour influences the behaviour of others. Our behaviour is what people see, and what others judge us by. We often don't know what drives other people's behaviour, but can, at vulnerable times, see it as something we have caused, as opposed to thinking, *"I really don't know what is going on for them, and I will have to make a decision, as to whether I choose to ask them about it or leave them be."* The key issue here will be not to put up with inappropriate behaviour, but to deal with this in an adult-to-adult manner, by asking 'what questions' rather than 'why questions'.

Our behaviour is the outward manifestation of our values, beliefs, assumptions, expectations and experiences. The effect of our behaviour can have immediate impact. For example, speech patterns in a new language will tend to follow those of your first language, and may convey incorrect messages to the listener. Maybe English, spoken by someone with staccato patterns of speech, will sound aggressive to the listener. This can add emotions to the message, which are not actually there, causing confusion and conflict. Add to this any preconceived notions you have about people from that culture, and you confirm the problem with that individual or group in your own mind.

Another example is what happens in a conflict situation. In conflict, some cultures prefer to use the inactive (passive/quiet) voice; for the person using the active (dynamic/vigorous) voice – this can exacerbate the situation.

In a conflict situation, depending on the culture you come from – community and family culture applies here – you may have learnt to use an inactive voice to resolve and work things out, or you may have learnt to use a dynamic voice to put your point across. When these two ways meet, it is not difficult to see how a conflict may be worsened.

Misinformation
Given wrong information about a situation, then making assumptions based on stereotypes, e.g. a person from another culture is late – you assume it's down to their being lazy/unpunctual; you then find out that their child was ill, and the doctor was late.

On holiday in the Gambia, a local guide said, "We also have GMT – Gambia Maybe Time". Now, some of the Gambian people were a bit 'chilled'; but, it would have been unhelpful had I gone on to view them all as tardy.

This can also be where you give out partial information which people from some cultures can easily fill in, because 'everyone knows that', but a person from another culture may not, and is thus excluded/set up to fail.

Expectations
Different cultures may expect people to act differently in a given situation, e.g. you learn of someone's illness; in some cultures, you would be expected to go over and do whatever you could to help them; in other cultures, that would be deemed intrusive –preferable that you phone, or send in a card, offering sympathy and any help they might ask for.

Integration into the dominant culture
For some individuals and groups, it is recognised that integration into a different cultural setting can be hastened if there are only a few individuals/groups from your own culture, because individuals/groups may need to adapt quickly.

Whereas, if there are many individuals/groups from your own culture, then it is likely that the individuals/groups will be slow to integrate, or may remain fairly separate. For example, in the London Borough of Tower Hamlets, there is a large Bangladeshi community, where some members are able to live their lives, barely touching upon any culture outside their own.

Assumption > Behaviour > Outcome

Model developed by Karen Murphy, Muika Leadership.

What are the outcomes, if the information we receive is not correct?
When the information we receive is not correct, then our assumptions and behaviours, which are associated with that information, are also incorrect.

When this information is about individuals and/or groups of people, who are not like us, might not look like us, might not like the same food, or have the same lifestyles or beliefs as ourselves, then our assumptions and behaviours, based in good faith on the information we have, serve to injure those people or misrepresent them.

If we look beyond these perceptions, then assumptions and behaviours, based on incorrect information, are also detrimental to us as individuals, because we are perpetuating this misinformation.

Some questions to ask yourself
- What assumptions do you hold, regarding diversity, inclusion and equality? Is it core to everything you do and believe in? Is it something you consider difficult to deal with? In the workplace, is it integral to everything that you do, or a 'bolt on', in addition to your 'day job'?
- What assumptions do you make about people who are 'different'? Do you embrace that difference, or do you think that, by being different, that person or group are somehow not as good as you i.e. inferior?
- How you view others who are different *will* be reflected in your actions and behaviours, whether you realise it or not, and so, the outcomes you get may not always be what you expect.
- How you view diversity, inclusion and equality will be reflected in your performance, whether you realise it or not.

Look at the model below to see how one negative experience or hearsay can have an impact.

Experiences

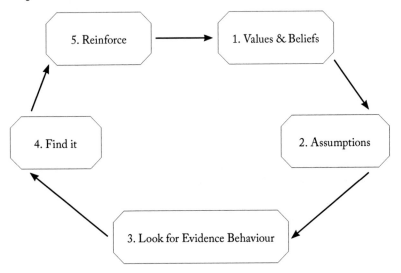

Left unchallenged, this behaviour pattern will self perpetuate.

Chapter Nine

Culture

"" *No culture can live, if it attempts to be exclusive.*
Mohandas Gandhi

- **The Power of Cultural Beliefs**
- **Cross Cultural Communication**

What is Culture?

The term culture refers to the system of assumptions, beliefs, sentiments and perspectives, many of them unconscious and taken for granted, which members of a group have in common. There can often be an overlap with religion. This can sometimes lead to confusion, where people claim that they are following some belief, because it is part of their religion, whereas it is in fact something which has grown up traditionally from their culture, and may not be practised by people of the same religion but who have a different culture.

Most, if not all cultures are in a state of change and development, and are affected and influenced by other cultures.

For example, there are statements, which are culturally conditioned, and which individuals/groups believe to be true, such as:

1. You should always be on time.
2. If someone upsets you, tell them.
3. Women should not wear make-up.
4. You should always refuse an offer the first time.
5. You should choose your own partner.
6. Polite men will allow women to walk through doorways first.
7. Individuals have the right to make decisions about their future, regardless of what their family wants.
8. A mother should not seek paid employment until the children are in full-time education.
9. Having a lighter skin tone is preferable.
10. Men don't/shouldn't express their feelings.
11. Speaking loudly in public isn't polite.

The Power of Cultural Beliefs

We are products of our family, culture, history and social environment. This means that it is the experiences from these groups, and those that we encounter in our day-to-day lives, that influence the way we behave, and the way in which we may respond to others. Our values and other people's values have a direct impact on the way we perceive ourselves, and the way we see others; the same is true for everyone. Those perceptions may be positive or negative. This is, in turn, given a more public form by the way in which we end up behaving. By being aware of what our values are, we can choose to behave in particular ways or not. Here are a few examples of cultural beliefs:

Slurping noises when eating may be considered a normal thing in some cultures whilst in others it may be regarded as bad manners.

In some cultures, looking someone directly in the eye is seen as a form of defiance and open dissent. However, in other cultures, it is seen as a common courtesy to look at people directly when you are speaking to them. (Just imagine how a situation might escalate, if two people with such opposing beliefs got into an argument.)

In some countries, it is considered very rude and improper, whilst sitting down, to show the soles of one's feet. (I once witnessed a woman remonstrating with some tourist for doing so in a temple.)

In some South East Asian countries, it is a sign of respect if you give someone their money by placing it down in front of them, as opposed to placing it in their hands. In Britain, we would expect the money to be placed in our hands. (Some people can give away their prejudice, by selecting into whose hands they are willing to place money.)

"Your enemy might become your friend, if you allow them to be who they are."

Cross Cultural Communication

"All culture and all communication depend upon the interplay between expectation and observation, the waves of fulfilment, disappointment, right guesses and wrong moves that make up our daily life."
E.H. Gombrich (1960) Art and Illusion.

In general, most of us speaking the same language have few problems in communicating with each other. If we are uncertain, or need more information, we simply ask. If this does not happen, we assume it is all clear.

This, however, may not be the case, where the people come from different cultural backgrounds. The problem is less when one or both of the parties know they have not understood, but rather when they wrongly think that they have understood correctly.

Most problems occur when people unconsciously attribute meanings to behaviours, based on their own ethnocentrism, thereby misreading them.

To avoid such problems, we need not only to gain knowledge of the other culture(s), but also to be aware of the influences our own culture and experiences (i.e. historical events) have on our own perceptions of life. This challenge increases in line with society becoming more multi-cultural/diverse/inclusive.

Cross-Cultural Communication

Message can be visual, verbal, or tactile

Deciding on the message – decisions, as to what messages need to be transmitted, are influenced by the sender's specialised and cultural meanings.

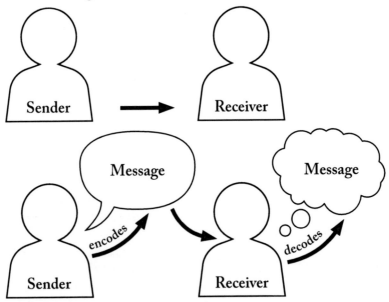

Encoding the intended meanings – this stage is determined by the sender's memory structure, language patterns and meanings that the receiver might not share.

Transmitting the message – this stage is influenced by the verbal communication habits, accents, or nonverbal behaviour.

Receiving the message – this stage is influenced by the receiver's habits of perception that are derived from their own specialised and 'cultural' identities.

Decoding and interpreting the message
This stage is influenced by the systems and structures of the receiver's values, beliefs, attitudes and behaviour that are derived from their own cultural background and experiences.

Inappropriate words and expressions
While all cultures have offensive terms for members of other cultures, religions, or ethnic groups, sometimes the offence is based not on the word, but more on its usage. Though people may avoid phrases or expressions which are openly offensive or racist, you will regularly hear examples of over-generalisations of a culture or ethnicity as having a particular characteristic, behaviour or quality – these will normally be negative.

Jargon, slang, metaphor
Jargon and slang, while readily familiar to people who have grown up in a country, may well form another barrier to minority groups who have not done so. Metaphors, jokes, satire all have aspects which command a high level of linguistic and cultural awareness to fully comprehend. Consideration needs to be given, when using such language, so as not to be exclusive.

Accent/Mispronunciation
Non-native speakers of English, especially those whose speech patterns, structures and sounds are significantly different to English, may well have accents which make their pronunciation of the language more difficult to comprehend. Any anxiety may additionally make them speak softly, and more stress is likely to make them speed up, compounding the difficulty.

Additionally, it may also be difficult to receive spoken English, especially as there are many regional accents, which may vary considerably from what the individual is used to hearing. Taking time to sensitively enquire that the person has clearly understood you will pay dividends. Remember times when you have been in another country and worked hard to understand what is being said to you and what a relief it is when a native speaker of the language is helpful and takes some time to help you.

Accent and Dialect are two elements of language. Language is one of the most important tools human beings have.

Accent refers to the way people pronounce words. Everybody has an accent. In all languages, with more than a few thousand speakers, you can find different accents within the same language.

Dialects are different forms of the same language, and usually the differences are regional, for example Cornish or Scots dialect. The main differences between dialects are usually in the actual words used to describe people, things or ideas, or in the way the words are arranged in sentences. There is no such thing as a good dialect or a bad dialect.

Standard English is the English dialect normally used in writing, for teaching, and heard on some radio and television stations. No accent or dialect is superior to another. Whether deliberately or accidentally, language can confuse, suppress and intimidate.

Body Language

Body language forms an important part of non-verbal communication, mostly operating on the subconscious level, which, like the spoken word, can have different meanings and significance across cultures, and thus be open to misreading. While issuing guidelines as to aspects of body language, which may well be widespread within a culture or which may be specifically different to our own, the very diversity within cultures tends to render such generalities as problematic as the very ignorance they attempt to replace. In all cases, don't assume – 'Check it out'.

The use of hand gestures is common and widespread, and one of the more conscious forms of body language, while the way you stand or sit can have great significance. The face, however, can have immediate impact, and most of its expressions remain on the less conscious level.

The eyes, they say, are the windows of the soul, and are inextricably linked with emotions, especially love; people set great store by their ability to 'read' another person through their eyes. Holding a gaze or looking away, depending on the culture, could signify honesty or shame, impudence or respect, dependent on the relationship, age or status of the two people.

When referring to children (or even adults), this holding or avoiding the gaze of another person is just as likely to come solely from what was expected by the parents, and may signify respect, as opposed to other commonly held assumptions of disrespect and/or rudeness.

The main or immediate issue is one of volume. In 'English culture', being loud is regarded as being angry, out-of-control, or common and boorish. As this may not be the case for people coming from other cultures, misinterpretation is rife in this area. In addition, the voice patterns of certain languages (Chinese, for example) can sound harsh, even aggressive to English ears.

All cultures have unspoken but clearly felt rules, as to proximity, body to body. Invasion of one's private space causes insecurity, annoyance or even aggression, or simply avoidance. Awareness and caution should be employed (see above).

As an extension to the above, some cultures or religions have strict codes about whom one may physically touch. Thus, they may not shake hands, particularly cross gender, or sometimes outside the immediate family. Even where handshaking is the norm, should it be firm and brisk, and how do you feel if it is limp, or lingers just slightly too long? Has the 'air kiss' developed, as a way of taking on the 'European style' without the contact? Whichever aspect of all of the above we consider, the general advice must be to remain aware, cautious, non-judgemental and, above all, welcoming and adaptable.

Self assessment and further considerations about culture are included in Chapter Thirteen

Chapter Ten

The Learning Cycle

Leadership and learning are indispensable to each other.
John F. Kennedy

The Learning Cycle

As life progresses, so does learning; it's natural and essential. If we accept this, it will help us to not shy away from, but embrace the journey. Organisations need always to be looking for ways to maximise the benefits of learning, both organisationally and individually; and, as individuals, we gain assurance from understanding how usual any discomfort may be, and that jumping back on to this learning progression is quite feasible.

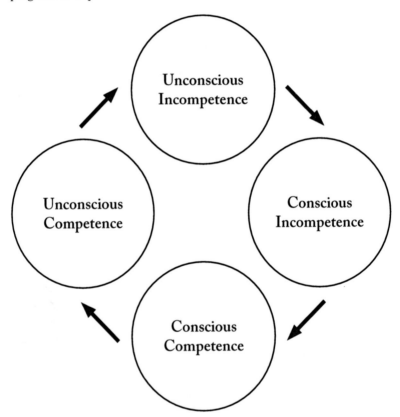

From Unconscious Incompetence to Unconscious Competence

In life, we go around fully aware that there are some things we are good at; that we just know; and there are others we don't. The problem comes with things we are totally unaware of, or (often worse) thinking we do know how to do it, or are even doing all very well – ignorant bliss. Shifting this state follows this pattern – a pattern we use in our training, and, at great depth, in Muika Leadership's 'Train the Trainer' programmes.

Firstly, you're in a state of *unconscious incompetence*, e.g. you use abusive language about and towards Travellers; you don't think about this, because your family and all your mates have always done so. *You don't know what you don't know.*

Then you get a job on the council, and become best mates with an older colleague, who quickly becomes to you the father you never knew. One day, in the pub, some of your old friends join you, and are soon bad-mouthing about the local Travellers site. When you join in, your new colleague and friend leaves quickly, without a word. The next day, he says how that mindset used to be him, but, since working closely with Traveller groups, he is a changed man. As he tells you more and more, you begin to see the error of your ways. You are now in the state of *conscious incompetence*: now, *you know what you don't know.*

With this new-found awareness, you make conscious decisions not to fall into old bad habits. After all, it took you a long time to build them up, so you do drop the occasional clanger. But, increasingly, you are able to see the potential error, before it is committed. You are at *conscious competence*: now, *you know what you know.*

Soon, you don't have to think about these new behaviours. They comfortably intermingle with all your other characteristics, maybe even altering some, which just don't quite fit any more. If you drive, you may remember the many tasks you had to do to get the car started, keep it going and bring it to a safe stop. Eventually, you reached a level of ability, where you could drive on regular routes to your destination, without any evident awareness of how you got there. You're in the state of *unconscious competence*. It's second nature for you to behave in this way – *you don't know what you know.*

Example – You feel you're ready to go up a grade at work; you have been eying up the position for some time now, and are quite sure you can handle it. In fact, it looks a doddle, with the current incumbent generally appearing totally 'chillaxed', as your children would say.

When he is promoted to another branch, you apply, and sail through the interview, happily accepting, when they offer you the post. The job's a breeze, so when, after a few weeks, you are called into the boss' office, you are expecting a quick, "How's it all going?" and probably a pat on the back for doing such a good job. It is then you are told how your section has fallen way behind, and other sections are having to take up the slack. What you had seen as a happy bunch of colleagues was actually correct, but only because you were being too soft on them and they had been taking advantage of you. You are told to go home, and tomorrow he'll let you know his decision. Overnight, you try to see exactly how you had messed up – and so quickly.

Thankfully, he sends you on a leadership training course, where you began learning about values and behaviour and specific leadership techniques, and very soon you become aware of just how inappropriate your style was. Yes, the staff liked you, but never learned to respect you, unlike your predecessor.

On returning to work, it was far from easy. Some of your colleagues tried it on with you at the beginning and you were taking time to get used to the new you, with your new skills, as much as they were. It felt to you a bit like trying to restart a personal relationship, when there was that awkward silence.

But, gradually, you started to get better in the job; learned how to say no. And the staff started responding in a positive way, in direct proportion to how reliably and naturally you utilised your new skills. Eventually, over time, someone could have looked in on that group, and seen a calm, cheerful and industrious place of work, just as it had been with your predecessor. Why, even your children didn't seem to be quite so testy.

The following diagram focusses on the issue of dealing with change, and how, for some, this can unbalance them. It is quite natural to feel concerned, when things change; however, by going back to your comfort zone, this may well prevent an individual or group from exploring opportunities, which would be better in the long run for self and others.

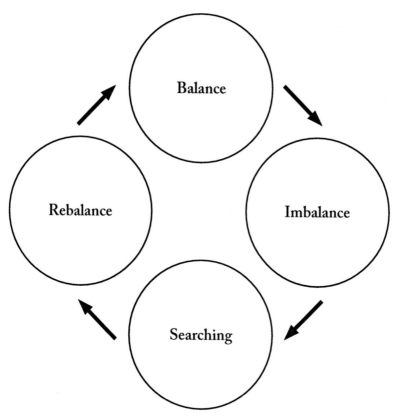

Balance

What we might refer to as our comfort zone; our place in the world, where we are settled, and know what we should do, and what we can expect.

Imbalance

Something new and different sets up a challenge to our knowledge, our beliefs, and our values and can uproot us to our very core, leaving us anxious, angry and confused – generally unbalanced. At this point, some of us will dismiss all this new stuff, and seek the safety of our old comfort zone. But, for us to move forward and develop, we need to get into the habit of questioning, not rejecting this new viewpoint.

Searching

Here, we take on the new information and see if we can verify it. Even where it may bring into question our long-held views, which we have always seen as facts, we will need objectively to assess this information, and see whether they can all live alongside each other, or if we need to dump one, even if it turns out to be one of our old ones. This will indeed be a healthy process for us, stopping us from becoming blinkered.

Rebalancing
This is where we start to integrate our new pieces of information alongside our other views and opinions, and readily utilise them, as they become fully known, owned and truly a part of us.

New Balance
Whatever we may have chosen to examine, adapt or adopt, this whole process will take us round to a different condition to where we began. It is our new comfort zone, our new balance.

An example

Balance
X is very comfortable in her current role and has learnt to manage her responsibilities.

Imbalance
X has been told that her current role is no longer applicable, and she needs to become a manager of nine people.

X goes home and tells her family about this change, and they talk about the concerns of managing a group of people she doesn't particularly get on with. So, X decides to look for another job, which is similar to the one she is doing. She doesn't tell anyone at work, but has lots of sleepless nights. Because she can't find another job, she then agrees to take on this new position.

Searching
X meets with her new team, and decides that they all need to meet once daily for a briefing, so that she knows what they are doing, having been told that a couple of them are very lazy, and don't take kindly to being told what to do. X goes home and has a row with her partner, saying that she dislikes the new job and all the responsibilities that go with it. Her partner, however, has just completed a leadership course, and recommends that she also sign up, to learn how to manage a 'dysfunctional' team. X now feels more confident, and decides to read a couple of books on leadership styles, and attends a learning and development programme.

Rebalancing

At this programme, she learns about herself and her lack of leadership qualities. Inspired by these revelations, she recognises that she has to take responsibility for her own behaviour, before she can ensure the other members in her team do. Armed with these new skills, she sets about having structured meetings and performance management appraisals.

New Balance

One year later, X is now much more confident in her worth as a leader, and has both the skills and knowledge required. Her team is no longer dysfunctional, and she enjoys her work. During this time, she occasionally finds that new changes are required for her to undertake; but now, she seems far more able to take them in her stride, and also is much more aware that the team respond far better to what they see her doing, than what she tells them to do.

I often use this model to start a learning and development session, because it provides individuals with an opportunity to think about how they manage behavioural changes – theirs or others. For example, a colleague might have given them some feedback about their behaviour towards women – do they change this behaviour for a short time, and then go back to their old habits, or are they confident enough to explore more about the impact they have on others?

The challenge for individuals and organisations is to have the time and opportunity to explore these issues together, and have them skilfully facilitated, so that everyone has the opportunity to explore their personal responsibility in any given action. Often, I hear that individuals have been promoted to managerial positions, without any training, and their leadership styles are based on 'how they like to be treated', 'how they have been managed before' or 'this is the way we do things around here'.

All this only perpetuates the status quo, as good or bad as it happens to be. Objective training and assessment for the new position opens up far greater potential for the individual and the organisation alike.

Chapter Eleven

Structures & Systems

> *Is the system going to flatten you out, and deny you your humanity, or are you going to be able to make use of the system to the attainment of human purposes?*
> Joseph Campbell

- **What's happening in your organisation?**
- **Organisational Policies and Practices**
- **Diversity & Inclusion Strategy, and Performance Management Framework**
- **Performance Measures**
- **Steering Committee**
- **Monitoring to Stop Discrimination**
- **Monitoring Form**

In this chapter, I set out policies, strategies and procedures which I have found to be invaluable to the successful running of a fair and inclusive organisation. At the time of writing, I see the public duty for doing this being weakened, while, for the private sector, it remains a recommendation. Yet, at a time of great financial pressure, I am assured that organisations which vigorously adopt these approaches, will stay safe, provide an inclusive environment for their staff, and thus prosper.

Organisations will be at different places – some will have policies, whilst others will not – some may say 'Why fix something which isn't broken?' – some may have rigorous monitoring, and learning and development programmes – some may have commitment and understanding from the Senior Leadership Team – some may already recognise the commercial benefits of ensuring diversity underpins all aspects of the company, and is the very DNA of the organisation.

There may well be individuals in the organisation, who are not prejudiced, but discriminate, based on *'This is the way we do things here' and/or (as I have often heard) 'This is more than my job's worth – I am not going to complain, because they may well be on my next interview panel'*.

There are also organisations which have discovered the business benefits of putting their policies into practice, and have a diversity and inclusion manager; but there isn't consistency of understanding about inclusivity across all departments within the organisation. I have also worked with diversity and inclusion managers, who have expressed frustration about individuals, and, specifically, managers' inappropriate comments and lack of understanding. I have also worked with highly committed and effective senior leadership teams, who model inclusive practices, have clarity of understanding, and work hard at ensuring all aspects of the business are inclusive. I have read vision, mission, and value statements with very fine words, but little evidence of putting them into practice.

The challenge for all organisations is to ensure diversity and inclusion is a business imperative, and that everyone is a champion and accountable.

The following information enables organisations to conduct self-assessments on their existing practices, though we recommend that an external organisation that specialises in diversity, inclusion and equality is employed to professionally audit and assess.

- What evidence is there to clearly demonstrate that your organisation advances recruitment and career paths, and reviews, monitors and evaluates the intrinsic value of diversity, inclusion and equality?
- When it comes to recruitment, promotion and board roles, what is the mindset of the decision makers?
- What are the 10 key factors that your organisation puts in place, with regard to diversity, inclusion and equality?
- Who makes the rules?
- What rules need to be altered, to ensure diversity, equality and inclusion?
- What assumptions are made about diversity, inclusion and equality?

Organisational Policies and Practices Should:

1. Acknowledge and value diversity, inclusion and equality;
2. Focus on how they will challenge stereotypes and assumptions;
3. Ensure that the achievement of all employees is not restricted because of their accent/dialect, age, colour of skin, disability, gender reassignment, marriage/civil partnership, pregnancy/maternity, race/ethnicity, religion or belief, socio-economics, sexual orientation (bisexual, gay, heterosexual, lesbian), etc.

Checklist for ensuring Diversity, Inclusion and Equality in the Workplace

- Acknowledge that all leaders are role models, and that their positive attitudes are fundamental to ensuring that we promote good relations between all groups, prevent all forms of unlawful discrimination and promote equal opportunities.
- Ensure that all employees comply with the equalities legislation, and have the confidence in preventing and challenging all forms of unlawful discrimination.
- Ensure that interventions in discrimination do not create fear and humiliation, but encourage understanding and clarity about the witting or unwitting behaviours.
- Ensure that everyone understands that the definition of an 'ism' is to "advantage or disadvantage someone because of their... age, disability, gender reassignment, pregnancy/maternity, marriage or civil partnership, race, religion or belief, sex and sexual orientation."
- Ensure that all documents, literature and displays avoid stereotypes, and celebrate differences and similarities.
- Ensure that inappropriate behaviour and language are effectively challenged and discussed in an atmosphere of openness.

- Ensure that everyone understands that collusion is unhelpful, dangerous, and limits potential.
- Whistle-blowing is encouraged in some workplaces, and clearly isn't understood in others – do individuals or groups collude with inappropriate behaviour, for fear of their own positions within the organisation? Or, do individuals and management understand that collusion is silence, active participation, as well as denial that victimisation and bullying is taking place. Some individuals suffer in silence – they may well leave, whilst others may confront the perpetrators.

Does your organisation have the following?

a. Does your organisation have a Single Equality Scheme, which describes, in a single document, how they will promote equality of opportunity, and avoid discrimination, demonstrating their commitment to placing the promotion of diversity, inclusion and equality at the centre of every aspect of their work?

b. Does your organisation's Single Equality Scheme demonstrate how they intend to meet the requirements of the Equality Act 2010, and implement these in an inclusive way, which takes account of all protected characteristics, including human rights?

Are all employees familiar with their duty of care to:
- promote equality;
- be proactive;
- seek to avoid unlawful discrimination before it occurs?

Are all employees aware of the legal ramifications of positive action and positive discrimination, and what the definitions are?
- Has your organisation agreed procedures for recording and dealing with all discriminatory incidents?
- Are all employees aware of procedures, and have these been reviewed, monitored and evaluated?
- What assumptions do people in your organisation hold, with regard to diversity, inclusion and equality?

Which of the following areas are people in your organisation less likely to understand, and, either wittingly or unwittingly, make inappropriate comments about?
- Age
- Class

- Disability
- Gender Reassignment
- Marriage/Civil Partnership
- Pregnancy and maternity
- Race
- Religion or Belief
- Socio-Economics
- Sex
- Sexual Orientation – Bisexual; Gay; Heterosexual; Lesbian
- Status
- Other

Diversity & Inclusion Strategy and Performance Management Framework

Diversity & Inclusion Strategic & Performance Management Framework

Builds on the principles of Quality, Leadership, Inclusion and Commitment

A framework that supports all aspects of Diversity & Inclusion

Systematic Approach

Integrate with existing initiatives

Putting Strategic Diversity & Inclusion Policies into Business Practices

The framework should be a systematic approach that brings about change, and requires a rigorous approach to verification and evaluation, as well as the identification of evidence to demonstrate strengths and gaps. All achievements should be regularly publicised in order to gain the confidence and trust of employees and other stake holders.

Diversity, inclusion and equality policy should contain a comprehensive and systematic approach to dealing with all diversity, inclusion and equality issues.

- Prevention – Learning and Development Programmes
- Interventions – clear guidelines on logging, investigating, recording and reporting all discriminatory incidents.

The overall aim is to provide an anti-discriminatory and anti-oppressive environment, where every individual takes responsibility for their behaviour, and a place where individuals feel appreciated, valued and understood.

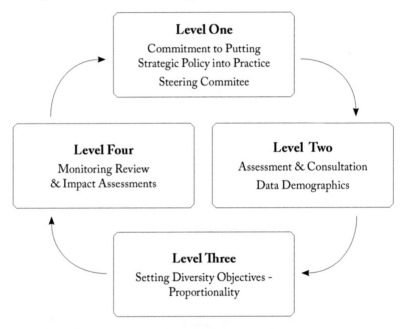

Level One Commitment to Putting Policy into Practice
Commitment from the:

- Top Team
- Board
- Senior Leaders
- Shareholders
- Partners
- Suppliers
- Sponsors

Steering Committee
The function of a steering committee is to assist in the implementation of the framework, and secure continuous and consistent improvement. It

needs to be authoritative, and have clear links to the corporate decision-making processes, including senior leadership teams and the board members. It should be chaired by a Chief Executive or member of the Senior Management Team.

The structure of the Steering Committee should include a diverse range of individuals, who have the range of skills and knowledge, as well as equality expertise.

Employees from all levels or tiers within the organisation, including part-time, shift and seasonal workers, should be encouraged to participate (this ensures an overview of the organisation's strengths, weaknesses and achievements, from a range of organisational perspectives).

Established power relations, such as line management, can undermine effective participation, and the Steering Committee should establish structures to overcome any potential barriers.

Transparent
Transparency encourages openness, and a willingness to drive the diversity and inclusion agenda forward. Clear messages should be given about the Diversity & Inclusion (D&I) Performance Management Framework.

Terms of Reference
- To ensure accountability within and across the organisation;
- To set the diversity and inclusion strategy and goals for the organisation;
- To make diversity and inclusion a reality for employees, clients, board members etc;
- To manage progress against specified plans and goals.

Key Responsibilities
- Provide strong leadership, consistency of approach and champion diversity and inclusion;
- All members to engage in learning and development programmes, to ensure a shared understanding of diversity and inclusion – policy and practice;
- Ensure the policy sets out clearly the principles, aims, objectives and action plan, for the promotion of diversity and inclusion, within the organisation;

- Ensure that the legal, business and ethical case for Diversity & Inclusion is clearly outlined;
- Influence positive change, by ensuring effective structures and systems, to enable the policy to be put into practice;
- Audit and assess diversity and inclusion performance and accountability, within all business areas;
- Ensure all learning and development programmes are underpinned by diversity and inclusion;
- Meet quarterly and annually to review progress.

Further questions to consider
- Have the right people been involved in the process?
- Do they have the knowledge, skills and understanding required?
- Is the Steering Committee diverse in their knowledge, experiences and understanding?
- Do they work together as a strong team, sharing the same vision about diversity and inclusion?
- Is a review of diversity and inclusion on the agenda of board meetings?
- Have you included external scrutiny of the policy and practices?

Are there clear guidelines, which set out:
- The Diversity & Inclusion Performance Management Framework;
- Structures and systems which ensure the policy is put into practice, and evidence can be demonstrated that this is happening;
- Business Area/Departmental self-assessment processes;
- Corporate validation of business areas; diversity and inclusion audits and assessments;
- Learning & Development Programmes;
- Annual Corporate Diversity & Inclusion review/audit with external validation.

Have the aims and implementation of the diversity, inclusion and equality policy been clearly defined in all documentation/activities, as follows:
- Employee Handbook
- Induction Programmes
- Leadership Courses
- Learning and Development Programmes
- Meetings

- On your website
- On the intranet
- Marketing literature

Level Two – Putting the Policy into Practice
- Top management commitment – being proactive in promoting equality and good relations between all individuals, preventing all forms of unlawful discrimination;
- Building diversity and equality into other policies, and relationship to other policies – linked to strategic plans;
- Recruitment and selection and exit interviews;
- Clear vision and strategy and sharing the vision;
- Employee involvement (including part-time staff and volunteers) and commitment;
- Communicating the purpose and an effective communications network;
- Communicating the expected results, and understanding the contributions required;
- Communicating the timing;
- Quarterly reviews and monitoring of the policy;
- Annual review – meeting on impact of the policy – updating and amendments.

Level Three Monitoring – Setting Diversity Objectives – Proportionality

Monitoring
Equalities monitoring plays an important role, by giving organisations the information they need to:
- Highlight possible inequalities;
- Investigate their underlying causes; and
- Remove any unfairness or disadvantage.

Equalities monitoring enables organisations to identify and address issues of inequality and discrimination, and is therefore a critical way of supporting and ensuring the implementation of diversity and inclusion. It is all but impossible for an employer to proactively address diversity, inclusion and equality without having accurate data on the workforce.

Employment monitoring enables organisations to look at the make-up of their employees, and compare this with the proportionality of the diverse groups within their company. Equalities monitoring is a way of looking at how human resources practices and procedures affect people with different needs, so that we can address any inequalities, and make sure everyone understands the legal, ethical and business case for diversity and inclusion.

Monitoring to Stop Discrimination

Equalities monitoring helps the organisation to identify when customs, practices and traditions have the potential to discriminate against certain individuals or groups. It assists in putting the diversity and inclusion policy into practice. It should only be used when there is clarity about the reasons for monitoring; for example, recruitment, progression, talent management, positive action programmes, under-representation of individuals from minority groups.

It ensures fairness and equal treatment according to needs. Certain individuals and groups may have specific needs, which ought to be taken into account. It shows the statistics of your employees/stakeholders is not personal information. Personal details are protected by law, and must not be used for anything other than statistics; hence the monitoring is anonymous and confidential.

Equalities monitoring provides information on where the organisation's strengths are, and where the gaps are, in relation to being an inclusive employer or service provider. It prevents assumptions about people who may look similar but are different.

It is vital that organisations produce guidance, and hold open briefings/meetings, about why they are monitoring – and what they will do with the information – in order to allay any fears employees might have about completing the monitoring form.

Guidance should include some of the following:

*The information you provide is **confidential**, and is protected by the Data Protection Act.*

Our organisation complies with the Data Protection Act, which requires us to ensure that all the information it holds is accurate and kept confidential.

The monitoring audit will be conducted through a combination of electronic and paper collection methods. The form will be sent electronically by employees, using x system via e-mail. The data will then be fed direct into the organisation's Human Resource Information System.

Access to the data provided will be restricted, and personal information will not be made available, when looking at the composition of the workforce.

No individual will be identified in any workforce monitoring report.

The purpose of monitoring is to:
- support our commitment to provide a diverse and inclusive workplace;
- measure the impact of our diversity, inclusion and equality policy, enabling us to analyse how our policies, procedures and decisions affect employees;
- identify the make-up of the workforce;
- establish how employees develop their careers; whether certain groups of staff make better progress than others, and question why and where some groups may not be accessing training, or other learning and development opportunities.

Equalities monitoring enables organisations to identify and address issues of inequality and discrimination, and is, therefore, a critical way of supporting and ensuring the implementation of diversity and inclusion.

Diversity Monitoring
The only justification for monitoring the workforce is if it will help identify discrimination, and ensure diversity, inclusion and equality underpin all aspects of the organisation's business values.

The information which you provide on the form is confidential, and is kept in accordance with the Data Protection Act 1998 and used for the purpose of monitoring.

Vigorous consideration must always be given to issues of confidentiality and to the meaning of data.

Guidelines on Monitoring
- What is the purpose of collecting this data?
- How will it be interpreted?

- What baseline will be used for comparison?
- What will happen as a result?
- Be clear – monitoring on its own does not improve diversity, inclusion and equality.
- Because of the small numbers of transgender workers, the risk of monitoring gender identity may likely outweigh the benefits.

Diversity Monitoring Categories (based on the 2011 census)
Please note that this form is optional. While there is currently no legal requirement on most organisations to monitor the workforce, this can help the organisation to assess whether the diversity policies are being put into practice, and what more might need to be done.

Use this form to support a diversity, inclusion and equality agenda in the workplace. In the Race section, it is most appropriate to add any specific ethnicities prevalent in your area e.g. Polish.

Age
☐ 16-25   ☐ 26-34   ☐ 35-43   ☐ 44-52   ☐ 53-59   ☐ 60-64   ☐ 65+

Disability
Do you look after, or give any help or support to family members or friends, because of either long-term physical or mental ill-health / disability?
☐ Yes   ☐ No

Do you consider yourself to be a disabled person?
Under the Disability Discrimination Act 1995, a person is considered to have a disability, if they have a physical or mental impairment, which has a sustained and long-term adverse effect on his/her ability to carry out normal day to day activities.
☐ Yes   ☐ No

Race

Asian
- ☐ Bangladeshi
- ☐ Chinese
- ☐ Indian
- ☐ Pakistani
- ☐ Vietnamese
- ☐ Other Asian background

(Specify)_____

Dual Heritage
- ☐ White & Asian
- ☐ White & Black African
- ☐ White & Black Caribbean
- ☐ Other Mixed background

(Specify)_____

Black
- ☐ Caribbean
- ☐ African
    - ☐ Somali
    - ☐ Other African
- ☐ Other Black background

(Specify)_____

White
- ☐ English
- ☐ Irish
- ☐ Scottish
- ☐ Welsh
- ☐ Other White background

(Specify)_____

Other
- ☐ Any other ethnic background

(Specify)_____

Marital Status
- ☐ Divorced ☐ Single ☐ Living with Partner
- ☐ Widowed ☐ Married or Civil Partnership

Gender Reassignment
Is your gender identity the same as the gender you were assigned at birth?
☐ Yes ☐ No

Do you live and work full time in the gender role opposite to that assigned at birth?
☐ Yes ☐ No

Do you feel able to discuss your gender identity with colleagues at work?
☐ Yes ☐ No ☐ With some people, but not all

Sex
☐ Female   ☐ Male

Religion or Belief
☐ Buddhist   ☐ Muslim   ☐ Christian   ☐ Sikh   ☐ Hindu   ☐ Jewish
☐ No Religion

☐ Other religion or belief (specify) _____

Sexual Orientation
How would you define your sexual orientation?
☐ Bisexual   ☐ Heterosexual   ☐ Gay   ☐ Lesbian

What existing data do you have (quantitative, qualitative, informative), with regard to the diversity profile of employers, partners, clients and shareholders?
- What data do you need to gather?
- What other sources of data are required?
- What trends or issues have been identified through the data?
- Have the 9+ protected characteristics been assessed, and has some consideration been given to multi-dimension (e.g. Black lesbians, older women, younger minority groups etc); what about socio-economics and poverty?
- What methods will be used for the gathering of the data, and how will they be clear and sensitive?

Level Four – Review & Equality Impact Assessments (EIA)
Do you need to carry out an EIA? Some questions to consider are as follows:

Does your policy/function affect people?
- Yes
- No

Is the focus on one or more of the following?
- Activities
- Functions
- Strategies
- Programmes and services or processes

Decide if any further assessment is needed

Impact

- positively
- negatively
on different individuals or groups in different ways

Will individuals have access to, or be denied access to a service, as a result of your policy, or changes you propose to make to existing services or functions?

- Will the implementation of your policy result in individuals being employed, a change in employee levels, or a change in terms and conditions, employer or location, either directly or indirectly?

If you have answered yes to any of these questions, your policy/function does affect people, and you should undertake an equality impact assessment.

- Name of the policy or function being assessed
- Names and roles of the people carrying out the Impact Assessment (Assessment Team)
- Statement on Aims
- What is the relationship to the organisation's vision and values?
- What are the Target Groups?
- How are profit/productivity increased?
- What are the existing data? Staff Profile/Customer Profile/Capabilities/Complaints/Exit interviews?
- What analysis has taken place? What are the findings?
- What action needs to take place? Why? Who? How? When?
- Executive Summary

Equality Impact Assessment

A successful EIA will look at four key areas

1. Policy – a clear definition of your policy and its aims;
2. Collecting evidence and engagement with diverse equality groups;
3. Differential Impact – reaching an informed decision on whether or not there is a differential impact on equality groups; at what level, and what you will do to address any adverse impact;
4. Measuring outcomes – stating how you will be monitoring and evaluating the policy/function, to ensure that you are continuing to achieve the expected outcomes for all groups.

Steps 1–10

Step 1
Define the aims of your policy/function

Step 2
What do you already know about the diverse needs and/or experiences of your target audience?

Step 3
What else do you need to know to help you understand the diverse needs and/or experiences of your target audience?

Step 4
What does the information you have tell you about how this policy/ function might impact positively or negatively on the different groups within your organisation and/or your clients/customers/service users?

Step 5
Will you be making any changes to your policy/function?

Step 6
Does your policy/function provide the chance to promote equality of opportunity, good relations between different groups, and prevent all forms of unlawful discrimination?

Step 7
Based on the work you have done, rate the level of relevance of your policy/function – HIGH, MEDIUM OR LOW

Step 8
Do you need to carry out a further impact assessment?

Step 9
Please explain how you will monitor and evaluate this policy/function to measure progress.

Step 10
Sign off, and publish impact assessment on your website

Chapter Twelve

Self-Assessment

 It is not the strongest of the species that survives, nor the most intelligent, but the ones most responsive to change.
Charles Darwin

- **Further questions for consideration**
- **Climate Mapping**
- **Displays**

Organisational Self Assessment

I have included further questions that will help organisations to carry out a review/assessment of their strengths and gaps. Some organisations may well be able to tick many of these, whilst others, who tick fewer, may well have exclusive practices which result in not reaching out to the potential talent available, and risk losing said talent, which is costly, both emotionally and financially.

Have any areas of potential adverse or differential impact been identified, in relation to the nine+ protected characteristics?

- Have current customs, practice and processes been analysed, to find the strengths and potential barriers/weaknesses?
- Is there evidence of disproportionate, adverse impact on some groups being recruited, retained or progressing within your organisation?
- What needs to happen in order to diminish disproportionate impact on individuals or groups who are different based on the nine+ protected characteristics?
- What consultation and involvement is required for change to happen?
- What recommendations are there for future assessments, such as monitoring and consultation?

Checklist – Key Questions

Do you regularly review and update your understanding of what may be considered direct or indirect discriminatory attitudes and behaviour, based on assumptions, because of someone's difference or similarity?:

- Age
- Disability
- Gender Reassignment
- Marriage and Civil Partnership
- Pregnancy and Maternity
- Race
- Religion/Belief
- Sex
- Sexual orientation i.e. bisexual; gay; heterosexual; lesbian

2. Do you have knowledge of, and information about, the diverse backgrounds of the people in your organisation, and, in particular, the ones you work with?

3. In your contact with all employees, do you aim to promote positive understanding and celebration of the diversity of contemporary society?

4. Do you check promotional literature and any displays for biased and stereotyped messages, and aim to use materials that accurately reflect the diversity of contemporary society?
5. Do you check your own assumptions before making assessments and judgements about employees?
6. Do you effectively challenge stereotyped assumptions, so that the 'ism' doesn't go underground?
7. Do you check the language you use, to avoid inappropriately loaded words that may reinforce stereotypes?

Resources and displays in the workplace, and the language, attitude and behaviour used, should not reinforce biased and negative stereotypes, but provide for employees, and those they work with, an opportunity to positively acknowledge and celebrate their own cultural identity whilst respecting the fact that individuals may not share their lifestyles but have the same basic needs that should be met, such as to be valued and respected; to feel understood and needed; to have the opportunity to give and receive attention; to feel a sense of control, and a clear and shared sense of purpose and goals.

Checklist

The challenge for individuals and all groups is to be proactive, with regard to diversity, inclusion and equality by:
- Being receptive and generous towards each other's identities, internally and externally, and being prepared to learn from them, as distinct from wishing to exclude or be separate;
- Challenging all myths and negative stereotypes, in a proactive and effective manner;
- Identifying prejudice and discrimination, and doing something about it, to make a positive difference for all, so that any barriers, self-imposed or institutionally imposed, are broken;
- Being open to change, choice and development, as distinct from being unreflective and rigid in values and beliefs;
- Ensuring that all functions, policies and procedures are inclusive and non-discriminatory;
- Ensuring the prevention or elimination of discrimination between persons, on grounds of human rights, equitability and fairness;
- Ensuring fair employment practices, with regard to recruitment, selection, retention, promotion and continuous professional development.

Climate Mapping

Climate mapping is about ensuring the workplace environment displays a healthy, discrimination-free zone for all employees. It is no good having all the policies and practices on diversity, inclusion and equality, if your employees, every day, work in rooms, and walk down corridors, which betray this positive aspect.

Look to ensure photos/paintings that may line your rooms and corridors reflect, where possible, a broad spectrum of your workforce. Do you have pictures displayed which strengthen old, established views of people, based on their difference? Put up images of people from diverse groups, in positions of power, or in other positions they are too often presumed not to be suitable for.

The key is to ensure your employees and clients feel comfortable and welcomed, whatever their background.

Displays

Display is not only a means of delivering knowledge, but also a major opportunity, to celebrate and acknowledge the richness of the diversity, lifestyles, positive experiences and achievements of all the people in the workplace.

Display is also a way of exploding 'myths' e.g. that only men are in management positions; that all professionals are White; and that people who have a physical disability are totally dependent on others. Displays of people of different appearances, facial features and sizes can help counteract negative, stereotypical images.

Again, this makes business sense – potential and existing clients will feel valued, appreciated and accepted for their difference, which is visually acknowledged.

You may wish to consider displays which:
1. Might provoke discussions about a variety of images, ages, appearances, sizes, heights and styles of dress;
2. Will reinforce an individual's sense of identity and belonging;
3. Show boys and men in nurturing and caring roles, and expressing their feelings (crying), and show women, not only as mothers and carers, but also celebrate their invaluable role in the workplace;

4. Depict areas considered to be male or female dominated, such as the construction industry or nursing, but with non-stereotypical workers;

5. Show women, Black people, lesbian and gay people, disabled people, as well as people from different socioeconomic backgrounds, who have achieved academically and scientifically;

6. Have positive images of a range of achievements, from regions in Europe and countries around the world.

Chapter Thirteen

Self-Assessment

> *Begin challenging your own assumptions. Your assumptions are your windows on the world. Scrub them off every once in a while, or the light won't come in.*
> Alan Alda

Further consideration about culture – assumptions, behaviour and outcomes

- **Eleven point guide to successful cross-cultural communication**
- **Approaches to working in a culturally competent workplace**
- **Examples of differences between cultures**

Eleven Point Guide to Successful Cross-Cultural Communication

1. Acknowledge that every human being has emotions, needs and feelings that are as sensitive as your own.
2. People are different, and will have their own perceptions of what they believe is normal, acceptable or unacceptable.
3. Understand and appreciate your own culture.
4. Be cautious about how you interpret other people's body language, in terms of your own values and beliefs, and personal and professional experiences.
5. Learn to cope with uncertainty. Avoid making assumptions about people who are different.
6. Looking different, not expressing the same preferences, does not mean being odd or to be avoided – there may be times when people need to agree to differ.
7. Don't make the assumption that what you are saying is received in the way you wished for. It is important to check it out in a positive and supportive manner.
8. Take care not to use jargon or phrases, which are understood only by certain people and, therefore, can be misunderstood.
9. Be aware of your own body language and facial expressions, and how these might be interpreted.
10. You may need to adapt your behaviour in response to the feedback you are getting.
11. Ask questions for clarification, in order to prevent misunderstandings.

Approaches to working in a culturally competent workplace

- Sensitivity to cultural variations, and the cultural bias of your own values and beliefs, inherited and learnt, through a diverse range of positive and negative experiences;
- Gain an understanding about the cultural knowledge of your work colleagues;
- Ability and commitment to developing an approach to ensuring your interpersonal skills and strategies reflect and are sensitive to the cultural needs of your colleagues;
- Ability to face increased complexity in working across cultures. This does not mean that such work entails more problems. On the contrary, a properly developed approach will enrich the experiences of all colleagues in the workplace;
- In particular, all interactions deal with the establishment of

boundaries. Individuals will bring expectations and beliefs, which will need to be made explicit.

Practical issues to consider:
1. How your culture or background affect your attitude to individuals/ groups, which are different to you.
2. Whether or not you see your colleagues' differences or similarities positively or negatively.
3. Whether or not you see the individual's culture as part of the solution to the present problem.
4. Whether or not you can accept, acknowledge and understand the individual's culture.
5. Whether or not your expectations about the individual's culture affects the atmosphere within the workplace.
6. Whether or not any cultural prejudice, experienced by you, affects your relationship with your colleagues.

Examples of differences between cultures might be:
- The relative significance of past or future events;
- The relative importance of traditional values;
- The differing obligations towards all members of the family;
- The use of rational, as opposed to intuitive or superstitious, ways of understanding events;
- The differing roles of women and men.

Skills required:
1. An ability to listen accurately to the extensive information that individuals across cultures offer.
2. Non-verbal skills – for example, can you adopt the most appropriate gestures, greetings and body language?
3. An ability to communicate and facilitate understanding across cultures.
4. An ability to focus on feelings, expressed in ways unfamiliar to your culture.
5. An ability to interpret accurately the expression of strong feeling outside your own culture, for instance anger, fear or grief.
6. An ability to recognise when a lack of expression of strong feeling by a colleague/s represents a cultural rather than an individual variation.
7. An ability to deal sensitively and effectively with the prejudices of colleagues and their effects, so that there is an effective working relationship.

8. Organisational skills – for example, deciding how and when to use resources – human/written/visual – when you are not conversant with your colleague's culture.
9. Ability to maintain and develop an understanding and knowledge about diverse cultures.

Further issues to be raised are:
1. How your own cultural status is perceived by your colleagues.
2. How your gender is perceived by people of the same gender or opposite.
3. Whether or not your sexual orientation is likely to increase or decrease your status in your colleague's culture.
4. Whether or not being older or younger is important enough in your colleague's culture to affect your status.
5. Whether or not your social and economic circumstances influence your status in your colleague's culture.
6. Whether or not your marital circumstances influence your status in your colleague's culture.
7. Whether or not your status is altered for your colleague/s, by your cultural and linguistic fluency.
8. How your colleague's culture sees your roles and responsibilities and job title.
9. Whether or not your religion or belief or political status influence others positively or negatively.

Chapter Fourteen

Delivering Training

> **"** *Common sense is the collection of prejudices acquired by age eighteen.*
> Albert Einstein

- **Muika Leadership and Focussed Thinking**
- **The Trainer/Facilitator: Self-awareness – social awareness**

Delivering training on diversity, inclusion and equality is vital, if there is to be a shared understanding about what this looks like and feels like.

Everyone has the potential to learn about themselves and others – they do not learn, if they are TOLD what to think and feel; they have to do this for themselves. Self-awareness is essential, as is social awareness, and underpins all skills and knowledge required in the workplace.

At Muika Leadership, we have created the concept of Leadership and Focussed Thinking.

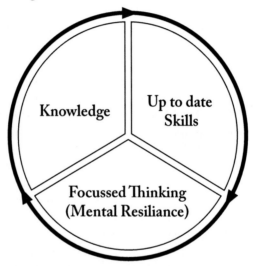

Focussed Thinking is a combination of how our minds work, and how to utilise the thinking, mindset and actions of highly successful organisations, where all aspects of business consider diversity, inclusion and equality.

It is no longer enough for diversity, inclusion and equality training to focus on the knowledge and skills of an individual. Of course, these are important elements; however, a major part of the success of an organisation is the process of Focussed Thinking, and the ability of the organisation's employees to perform this.

To ensure that individuals check the assumptions behind their thinking, and take responsibility for the resulting behaviour, we recommend that anyone delivering training has the following core competences:

The Trainer/Facilitator understands and knows:

about how their own cultural experiences and knowledge affect their assumptions, beliefs and behaviours;

1. the impact of their personal appearance, dress and physical positioning, in relation to trainees; hand and body movements, positioning of tables and tone of voice, on both the quality of the presentation and receptivity by trainees;
2. how to use a variety of self-management strategies to reduce personal stress and stage fright, associated with public speaking;
3. the potential impact of having been mandated to attend training; and can use supportive engagement strategies to help participants identify personal learning objectives, and develop an investment in the training;
4. they can create and orient participants to a comfortable physical learning environment, including preparing the training room, greeting and engaging trainees, and attending to the social, emotional and comfort needs of the learners;
5. how to use introductions and other activities at the beginning of a session to create a positive group climate, and begin the engagement process;
6. how to determine the training strategy best suited to meet a particular learning objective; and knows how to integrate a variety of strategies, to address different learning styles, and to keep the training from becoming repetitious or boring;
7. the typical stages in the development and management of new knowledge and skills; understands the adult learning paradigms that represent these steps i.e. levels of learning, conscious/unconscious competence;
8. a variety of group management strategies, and can intervene to manage problematic behaviours, without alienating either the individual or group;
9. how to clearly and accurately communicate the goals and objectives of the training; can help participants identify unrealistic expectations for the training; and can negotiate to achieve consensus about the desired outcomes for a training session;
10. the impact of individual learning preferences and culturally based learning styles, and can design a variety of teaching and transfer strategies that address different styles;
11. how they can incorporate content and examples that enhance participants' understanding of and comfort with the cultural issues inherent in the topic area being trained;

12. strategies to keep the group thinking focussed, on task, and within established time frames, while remaining responsive to group needs and concerns;

13. how to stimulate and facilitate discussion of emotionally-charged topics and issues during the training, and can monitor and manage the emotional level of the group, to maintain a safe, objective and comfortable training environment;

14. how they can facilitate discussions of assumptions, bias and stereotyping, and its negative impact on cross-cultural interactions, and can incorporate culturally relevant information into the training;

15. they can provide timely, sensitive and relevant feedback to the group, and can challenge ideas, in a manner that stimulates creative thinking, and promotes growth, while maintaining participants' self-esteem;

16. how to effectively handle confrontation and conflict, with and between participants; and can use a series of verbal and non-verbal interventions to de-escalate the conflict, explore and clarify the issues, and facilitate resolution, while discouraging disruptive behaviour, and preventing emotional withdrawal;

17. they can identify that cultural misunderstanding and expressions of discrimination may be contributing to interpersonal conflict in the training, and can use a variety of strategies to explore and resolve conflicts;

18. they can use reflective coaching, listening and feedback to encourage individual and group involvement, to clarify and expand upon contributions, to guide the direction of the discussion, and to enhance the participants' understanding of the content and concepts;

19. how they can use summarisation, bridging and segue to help preserve continuity, when moving between segments of the training;

20. how to clarify points, and determine the level of understanding or agreement.

Chapter Fifteen

Equalities Legislation

> *I do not want my house to be walled in on all sides and my windows to be stifled. I want all the cultures of all lands to be blown about my house as freely as possible. But I refuse to be blown off my feet by any.*
> Mohandas K. Gandhi

- **Background information to The Equality Act 2010**

Websites for further reference and information

Equalities Legislation

Age Discrimination – October 2006
The regulations apply to employment and vocational training. They prohibit unjustified, direct and indirect age discrimination, and all harassment and victimisation, on grounds of age, of people of any age, young or old.

Disability Discrimination Act 1995
The DDA prohibits discrimination against disabled people, in the areas of employment, the provision of goods, facilities, services and premises, education; and provides for regulations to be made to improve access to public transport.

The Disability Equality Duty (DED) – Came into force in April 2007
Focuses on institutional change, rather than individual, reasonable adjustments.

The DED will require all public sector organisations to publish a Disability Equality Scheme. The thrust of the DED is progression towards long-term cultural change, with the main characteristic of the Duty being a move away from a compliance-driven approach, towards one that is more proactive and anticipatory, in meeting the needs of disabled children and adults.

…."a physical or mental impairment, which has a substantial and long-term adverse effect on their ability to carry out normal day to day activities… they must have had the condition, or are likely to have the condition, for 12 months or more." Disability Discrimination Act 1995. Disability Discrimination Act 2005

The Act places a duty on all public bodies to promote disability equality. Disability Equality Scheme 2006

Public authorities to actively involve disabled people in how the sector works.

Included as active partners, rather than interested onlookers.

A legal duty to involve disabled people in planning its mechanisms, processes and environments.

Gender Equality Duty – Part of the larger Equality Bill April 2007
Gender Equality Schemes April 30 2007
Promoting gender equality effectively means a fundamental re-think in the design and delivery of services, as well as having implications for employment policy and practice. Those who get it right will reap the benefits in terms of improved customer satisfaction and employee productivity.

The duty to pay due regard to eliminating unlawful sex discrimination, and promoting equality between women and men, will apply to all public authorities. This is known as the 'general duty'. The general duty will also apply to voluntary and private sector bodies that are acting in a public capacity.

Race Relations Act 1976
The RRA makes it unlawful to treat a person less favourably than another on racial grounds. This covers grounds of race, colour, nationality (including citizenship), and national or ethnic origin.

Sex Discrimination Act (as amended) 1975
The SDA (which applies to women and men of any age, including children) prohibits sex discrimination against individuals, in the areas of employment, education, and the provision of goods, facilities and services, and in the disposal or management of premises.

Sex Discrimination Act – The Equal Pay Act 1970 (Amendment) Regulations 2003 – The Equal Pay Act 1970 (Amendment) Regulations 2004
Men and women should be given equal treatment, in the terms and conditions of their employment contract, if they are employed on:

- 'like work': work that is the same or broadly similar;
- work rated as equivalent, under a job evaluation study, which must be a proper analysis of the demands made on employees in their jobs, under various headings, such as effort, skill and decision making, and impartial in its application to men and women; or
- work found to be of equal value.
  A person discriminates against a woman, in any circumstances relevant for the purposes of any provision of this Act, if:

(a) on the ground of her sex, (s)he treats her less favourably than (s)he treats, or would treat a man, or

(b) (s)he applies to her a requirement or condition, which (s)he applies or would apply equally to a man, but which:

　(i) is such that the proportion of women who can comply with it is considerably smaller than the proportion of men who can comply with it, and

　(ii) (s)he cannot show to be justifiable, irrespective of the sex of the person to whom it is applied, and

　(iii) is to her detriment, because she cannot comply with it.

The Employment Equality (Sex Discrimination) Regulations 2005 amend the Sex Discrimination Act 1975 and Equal Pay Act 1970, so that they are compatible with the requirements of European legislation.

Discrimination on the ground of pregnancy or maternity leave
In any circumstances, relevant for the purposes of a provision, to which this subsection applies, a person discriminates against a woman if:

(a) at a time, in a protected period, and on the ground of the woman's pregnancy, the person treats her less favourably than (s)he would treat her, had she not become pregnant; or

(b) on the ground that the woman is exercising, or seeking to exercise, or has exercised or sought to exercise, a statutory right to maternity leave, the person treats her less favourably than (s)he would treat her, if she were neither exercising nor seeking to exercise, and had neither exercised nor sought to exercise, such a right.

Sex Discrimination (Gender Reassignment) Regulations 1999
These regulations are a measure to prevent discrimination against transsexual people, on the grounds of sex in pay, and treatment in employment and vocational training. They effectively insert into the SDA a provision to extend the Act, insofar as it refers to employment and vocational training, to include discrimination on gender reassignment grounds.

The Race Relations Act 1976 (Amendment) Regulations 2003 implement the EC Article 13 Race Directive.
The Regulations enhance the RRA by, for example, amending the

definition of indirect discrimination, and changing the way in which the burden of proof applies, as well as removing a number of exceptions from the legislation. The Regulations extend protection from discrimination on the grounds of race and ethnic or national origins. These apply in the fields of employment and training, social protection and social advantage, education, the provision of goods, facilities and services, and housing.

Race Relations (Amendment) Act 2000

The RR(A)A outlawed discrimination (direct and indirect) and victimisation in all public authority functions not previously covered by the RRA, with only limited exceptions. It also placed a general duty on specified public authorities to promote race equality.

It would be most remiss here, if we were not to highlight the great significance for race equality arising from a tragic event. The Stephen Lawrence Inquiry Report, chaired by Sir William Macpherson, led to some important changes in race equality legislation; the most ground-breaking being the definition of a racist incident: "any incident perceived to be racist by the victim or another person."

This came about because of a number of cases where people's reporting of incidents or crimes as having a racist element to them had previously been ignored, often leading to an escalation of intensity, sometimes resulting in death.

Employment Equality (Sexual Orientation) Regulations December 2003

These regulations outlaw discrimination (direct discrimination, indirect discrimination, harassment and victimisation) in employment and vocational training, on the grounds of sexual orientation. The regulations apply to discrimination on grounds of orientation towards persons of the same sex (lesbians and gays), the opposite sex (heterosexuals) and the same and opposite sex (bisexuals).

Employment Equality (Religion or Belief) Regulations December 2003

These regulations outlaw discrimination (direct discrimination, indirect discrimination, harassment and victimisation) in employment and vocational training, on the grounds of religion or belief. The regulations apply to discrimination on grounds of religion, religious belief or similar philosophical belief.

Human Rights Act 1998

The Human Rights Act came fully into force on October 2, 2000. It gives further effect in the UK to rights contained in the European Convention of Human Rights.

The Act:

Makes it unlawful for a public authority (e.g. government department, local authority or the police) to breach Convention rights, unless an Act of Parliament meant it could not have acted differently.

Means that cases can be dealt with in a UK court or tribunal. Says that all UK legislation must be given a meaning that fits with the Convention rights, if that is possible.

Promote good relations between people of different groups

Specific and positive action needs to be taken on a regular basis, to ensure adults:

- develop positive attitudes and behaviour to all people, whether they are different from or similar to themselves;
- unlearn any negative attitudes and behaviour that they may have already learnt;
- value aspects of other people's lives equally (such as their age, disability, gender, skin colour, physical features, culture, language religion or belief, sexual orientation), rather than seeing them as less worthy than theirs, or ranking them in a hierarchy.

I hope that you have found this book useful. However, I believe that people can have all the knowledge and skills about diversity, inclusion and equality, but it is how they use this information that matters.

If you know about this information, but do not implement it into your everyday behaviour, you may find you do not create the inclusive culture that supports every individual to perform to the best of their ability.

Websites for further reference and information

www.fawcettsociety.org.uk

www.runnymedetrust.org

www.irr.org.uk

www.idea.gov.uk

www.acas.org.uk

www.equalityhumanrights.com

www.equalityhumanrights.com/scotland

www.equalityhumanrights.com/wales

www.nihrc.org

www.edf.org.uk

www.cipd.co.uk

Testimonials

Mui Li is an expert in her field who understands individuals and organisations, communicates with authority and passion and connects with people emotionally and intellectually.
Professor Binna Kandola OBE, Pearn Kandola

Mui Li is a skilled practitioner in equality and diversity training. Her flexible, pragmatic approach to training and development ensures that all who are on the training programme are fully engaged with the course, and will derive the maximum benefit from the training.
Group Captain John Whitmell Provost Marshal (Royal Air Force)

Mui Li brings amazing energy and insight to her training work, and models beautifully what she teaches. An inspirational trainer.
Helen Howard, Collaborative Lawyer and Mediator

Mui is an outstanding trainer and coach. I found her to be truly inspiring and motivational. Her methods are thought provoking and outcome focused. I am honoured to provide this testimonial for Mui, and can't praise her enough for the difference her approach and training has made to so many people.
Muriel Awais-Dean, Manager and Lead Practitioner, Children's Services

I have had experience of Mui's coaching and mentoring services, and have been very impressed with her, and the high calibre quality of the women she has assisted professionally. I highly recommend her.
Davida Marston, Non Executive Director,
Mears Group PLC (business partner)

About the Author
Mui Li MA BA (Hons) PGCE

Born in North London to a Russian mother and Chinese father,
Mui grew up experiencing difference on a very personal level. From the
stories told by her parents about the Cultural Revolution, Stalin, Taoism,
Confucius and the Boxer Rebellion, to the conscious and unconscious
bias and 'polite prejudice' she experienced – where individuals felt it was
okay to make inappropriate comments. The firm grounding of self-worth,
instilled by her parents, and her continual personal and professional
development has enabled her to be confident, thus minimising any
negative effects of the discriminatory behaviour towards her.

Mui is now considered to be one of the leading experts in the field of
diversity, inclusion and equality, and has been involved in consultancy and
training for the past 20 years. Her previous roles, as teacher, advisory teacher,
curriculum leader and Education Officer, Director of Mui Li Associates,
and now co-founder of Muika Leadership, have led her to become one of
the most respected and sought-after speakers on this subject.

She has worked extensively with different organisations from the private
and public sectors, and is proud to say that the impact of her interventions
is always exceptionally positive, leaving the participants/organisations
enlightened, enriched, and motivated to bring about change.

Lightning Source UK Ltd.
Milton Keynes UK
UKOW052105130412

190708UK00001B/6/P

9 781907 722981